I Was Raised A Jehovah's Witness

Joe Hewitt

ACCENT BOOKS
Denver, Colorado

Fourth Printing 1986

AĆENT BOOKS

A division of Accent Publications, Inc.
12100 W. Sixth Avenue
P.O. Box 15337
Denver, Colorado 80215

Library of Congress Catalog Card Number: 78-73255

ISBN 0-89636-018-0

Contents

1 "The End Is Near"   5

2 In "The Truth"   19

3 "Enduring Faithfully to the End"   28

4 A Void in My Heart   39

5 Filling the Void   49

6 It Had To Be By Grace   57

7 The Society Strikes Back   65

8 "As One Dead"   74

9 Mama Got Her Wish   85

10 Doing Away with Hell   92

11 A Thimbleful of Understanding
   About the Trinity   107

12 The 144,000: Are There Classes
   of Salvation?   117

13 Transfusion: "Don't Eat the Blood"   130

14 Does Jesus Christ Make Two Gods?   137

15 What Is God's Name?   150

16 What Happens to the Soul at Death?   159

17 Then There Is "New Light"   166

18 The Christian's Duty as a Citizen   170

19 The Literal Return of Jesus Christ   176

20 Put on the Armour of God   183

1
"The End Is Near"

At the age of ten I stood on street corners selling *The Watchtower* magazine. I was trained in the "Theocratic ministry," and made my first public talk to an audience of two hundred at age eleven. I faithfully went from door to door placing the Watchtower Bible and Tract Society's magazines and books. Like a begging deaf-mute, I handed my testimony card to each person who answered the door. Without my having to say anything, the card proclaimed me to be a "minister of the gospel." The windup phonograph I carried spoke in a tin voice a recorded message by Judge Joseph Rutherford.

My experience as a member of "Jehovah's Witnesses" really began two generations earlier when my maternal grandfather, John Gordon, who farmed cotton in north Texas and across the Red River in what was then called Indian Territory, became interested in the teachings of Charles Taze Russell, founder of the Watch Tower Society, who believed that the Millennial Kingdom of Christ was dawning.

Russell was raised in a Congregational church, but at an early age rejected "organized religion." At the age of eighteen he organized a Bible class in Pittsburgh, which six years later in 1876 elected him "Pastor." The title stuck, and Jehovah's Witnesses still refer to him affectionately as "Pastor Russell" (though they generally reject the title for others, calling their equivalent official the "Congregational Servant").

Twenty-one years later the Watch Tower Society was firmly established. By the time my mother was born near Henrietta, Texas, in 1899, the youngest of six children, Russell was already predicting that Christ would return in 1914.

During the early years of the "Millennial Dawn" movement, congregations were called "Bible Student Ecclesias," using the Greek word "ecclesia" which meant assembly, or church, instead of "church." Many of the people who affiliated with these congregations believed and trusted in Jesus Christ as Lord and Saviour, and considered themselves to be born-again children of God. I believe my grandfather was one of these.

Early in its history the Watch Tower Society became known for predicting the Battle of Armageddon and *The End.* Yet the predictions never came true. An organization that has complete control over the minds of its disciples can make erroneous predictions and cancel them, one after the other, out of the minds of their followers after each failure of fulfillment like clearing an adding machine. And it can continue right on convincing them again and again that Armageddon is just around the corner.

This was the case with the Watch Tower Society. For example, in the January, 1886, *Watch Tower,* page 817, Russell said, "The outward evidences are that the marshalling of the hosts for the battle of the great day of God Almighty, is in progress while the skirmishing is commencing."

In 1889, Russell said in *The Time Is At Hand*, page 101, "... The battle of the great day of God Almighty (Rev. 16:14), which will end in A.D. 1914 with the complete overthrow of earth's present rulership, is already commenced."

In 1894, he said "skirmishing is already beginning ...." In 1904 he said the "great time of trouble" would culminate in October of 1914.

The May 1, 1914 *Watch Tower* said, "There is absolutely no ground for Bible students to question that the consummation of this Gospel age is now even at the door . . . ."

Then, as the year of 1914 began to wane, Russell started to soft-pedal and prepare his people for a possible letdown, when in the September 1, 1914 issue he said, "While it is possible that Armageddon may begin next Spring, yet it is purely speculation to attempt to say just when. We see, however, that there are parallels between the close of the Jewish age and this Gospel age. These parallels seem to point to the year just before us—particularly the early months."

In 1915 he said World War I, then raging, would lead to the Battle of Armageddon, which ". . . will be a great contest between right and wrong, and will signify the complete and everlasting overthrow of the wrong, and the permanent establishment of Messiah's righteous kingdom . . ." (*Watch Tower Reprints,* VI, April 1, 1915, page 5659).

A series of court trials showed that Russell owned the Society. He received publicity on his separation from his wife in 1897, and their separation decree in 1903, after a court fight in which it was revealed that Russell held 990 of the 1,000 capital shares in the Society (*Brooklyn Daily Eagle,* Nov. 1, 1916).

Other events took place that cast a shadow on Russell's honesty. The "Pastor" advertised "Miracle Wheat" for sale through *The Watch Tower* magazine at $1 a pound, claiming it would grow five times as much as any other wheat. The *Brooklyn Eagle* publicized the wheat offer and poked fun at it in an editorial cartoon. Russell sued for $100,000 damages. The newspaper declared at the beginning of the lawsuit that it would show that Pastor Russell's religious cult was nothing more than a money-making scheme.

In the course of the trial, government agents testified that there was nothing superior, let alone miraculous, about Russell's expensive wheat, and the *Eagle* won the lawsuit. Witnesses claim that all the proceeds of the wheat sale went to the Watch Tower, but Russell owned 99 percent of the Watch Tower, so he was making contributions to himself. His organization steadfastly refused to reveal financial details.

Russell died in 1916 without seeing the fulfillment of his predictions. My mother spoke with awe of Russell's death. She said he had been aboard a train in Texas when he became aware that he was about to die, and in preparation he had himself wrapped in a white sheet. Mama felt that the way he died was an indication of Russell's special contact with God.

A former Missouri judge, Judge Joseph Rutherford, was the Watch Tower Society's legal counsel at the time. According to William J. Schnell, author of *Thirty Years A Watchtower Slave* (Baker Book House, Grand Rapids, Michigan, 1971), Russell had made a will clearly leaving the leadership to others, but Rutherford, by deft corporate political maneuvering, garnered proxy votes, got himself elected president, and took control.

Rutherford published a book in 1920 entitled *Millions Now Living Shall Never Die,* which was purported to contain "New Light." Some of this *New Light* was a prediction of the end: ". . . The old order of things, the old world, is passing away . . . 1925 shall mark the resurrection of the faithful worthies . . . . We are standing at the very portals of that blessed time!" (pages 97 and 105).

Other *New Light* established the doctrine: only a few could be "born again" and go to heaven.

The old Russellites had considered themselves eligible for heaven, and at Russell's funeral, Rutherford had said, "Our brother sleeps not in death, but was instantly changed from the human to the divine nature, and is now forever with the Lord."

The hope of heaven had been arbitrarily jerked away from the rank and file; according to the *New Light* the average person hadn't a chance of heaven. Thus began the split between the Russellites, or *Millennial Dawnists,* who refused to go along with Rutherford's *New Light,* and those followers who accepted Rutherford's pronouncement like a good Catholic accepts the Pope's. The split occurred too in John Gordon's family.

The two oldest sons, my Uncles Jim and Al, went with the new order. The youngest son, Alfred, convinced that the followers of Rutherford denied that Jesus was the Son of God, stayed nominally with the Millennial Dawnists for a time, married a Methodist, and gradually drifted away from the Russellite beliefs. His children became Baptists. John Gordon's three daughters married and went the ways of their husbands. My father, Joseph Benjamin Hewitt, was the son of an atheist, whose father was a Methodist preacher. My father's atheism influenced the youngest daughter, my mother, away from any religious practice.

Grandfather Gordon continued to be identified with the Russellites, but his was a more personal faith, according to family members who saw him die. On his deathbed he cried to Jesus, calling Him Lord and Saviour. Confident that he would shortly be with the Lord, he said, "Lord Jesus, I'm ready to go."

Mama was impressed by Russell's faith. She was impressed by her father's faith. She felt deep within her heart that her father had found the Way.

During twenty-one years of marriage to my father, my mother made few attempts to find spiritual fulfillment. She lost touch with the religion of her father and was unaware of the 1925 prediction, and of Judge Rutherford's other enticements to his followers to urgently work because the time of *The End* was at hand. In 1929 he said the time of *The End* was close because the Jews were returning to Palestine (*Life*, page 170, 332). In 1930 he said, "The great climax is at hand" (*Light*, II, page 327).

In 1931, the year I was born at Grants, New Mexico, Rutherford said: "His day of vengeance is here, and Armageddon is at hand and certain to fall upon Christendom, and that within an early date. God's judgment is upon Christendom, and must be shortly executed" (*Vindication*, I, page 147).

When my parents' marriage was nearing its end, we were living on an eighty-acre farm deep in the woods of Boone County, Arkansas, near the tiny burg of Bergman. We lived in a four-room rough lumber house, which Daddy had built with his own hands from timber cut from the virgin forest.

Situated in a shallow valley surrounded by tree-covered hills, the little town of Bergman was cut in two by a gravel and rock-lined washout, spanned by a single heavy wooden bridge minus side rails. During business hours, horses were often seen hitched to the smooth wooden hitching rail in front of the Bergman Post Office.

The most exciting time for me to be in Bergman was when the train came through. Black, hot, belching black smoke and white steam, shaking the earth, and piercing the air and hurting my ears with long blasts of its shrill whistle, it usually snatched the Bergman mail sack off a pole at the depot, without slowing down.

There were two stores: one was built entirely of rounded, beige and rust native stones, and the other was of typical Western America frame construction, with a rectangular facade extending from the top of the wide porch to the peak of its pitched roof. During the Depression days of the '30s it was a rare treat for me as a barefoot kid to go inside and tread the worn smooth plank floor, taking in the blended aromas of freshly ground coffee, new fabric, and a wonderful collection of candy smells, to spend a penny.

Oblivious of religious concern, my world was playing in the deep washout, climbing stacks of railroad ties near the depot, exploring the woods, wading the clear water of the many creeks, and climbing trees, cliffs, and bluffs. Little did I know of the intricacies of adult life.

Daddy often was gone several days at a time in his work for the Harrison, Arkansas, *Boone County Headlight* weekly newspaper, and in his trading (he would buy and sell anything) and partying. Sometimes when he was at home he and Mama would have "words." Daddy was authoritarian, and the king of his home. So the "words" were mostly one way. One of Daddy's rules was that Mama could never go to "any d_____ church." Any time she did, she could "get out." That was the same rule his father, Benjamin Tarrant Hewitt, had given his wife. (As soon as he had died, my grandmother became a Baptist.)

I remember two experiences involving church.

About a mile from our home in the woods was the Oregon Flats Baptist Church. Beside a sandy dirt road, it was built of a jigsaw puzzle of flat flagstones, ranging in color from tan to dark red. In my memory there was always a crescent cushion of pink and white flowers between the surrounding woods and the green lawn of the churchyard. It was what the ideal country place of worship would seem. But inside, to a little boy to whom church was strange anyway, it was contradictory: the Sunday school was pleasant; they told Bible stories, none of which I remembered, and gave me a pretty, colored picture card to take home. But after Sunday school everybody gathered in the main auditorium and the preacher got red in the face, shook his fist and yelled what were to a four-year-old, big, strange words. One experience of that was enough. I never again stayed for church.

The other experience was at a Methodist Church in Bergman on Mother's Day. As we entered the white frame church building, my sister Rose Ellen and I were given red roses, and my mother was given a white one. When I asked why, Mama explained that she wore the white rose because her mother was dead. She had died of tuberculosis when Mama was only eight. It was a shock to me to think that some-day my mother might also die.

I was not sure what everything meant when Germany invaded Poland in 1939, but the electric tension was transmitted from the adults to the children. People were fearful of war. The Society capitalized: ". . . The time for the battle of the great day of God Almighty is very near . . . The disaster of Armageddon is just ahead" (*Salvation*, pages 310, 361). In 1940, Rutherford said "The prophecies of Almighty God . . . show that the end of religion has come and with its end the complete downfall of Satan's entire organization" (*Religion*, page 336). "The witness work for THE THEOCRACY appears to be about done in most of the countries of 'Christendom' " (*The Watchtower*, Sept. 1, 1940, page 265). This was an allusion to Matthew 24:14, which every Witness could quote, "And this gospel of the kingdom shall be preached in all the world for a witness unto all nations; and then shall the end come."

At those times we were unaware of Rutherford's continuing predictions, but we listened to the radio, and fear was expressed especially for the young men who might get drafted and have to go to war.

Out in the country it was unusual to have visitors, so I remember well the woman, carrying what looked like a small suitcase, walking up the road to our house. I kept about my business of playing around the smokehouse with my mostly-collie dog, named Fat, but did take note of the occasion. The lady came back many times on other days. She carried a satchel with many colorful books and pamphlets, and the small "suitcase" turned out to be a phonograph on which she played the voice of an unseen man speaking, what were to me, big, strange words.

"Are you sure this is what my father believed?" Mama asked the visitor, who eagerly assured her that it was. Later I remember Mama telling people how she was now satisfied that she had found what her father had believed.

Daddy sold the farm, and moved us into Bergman in a house that was surrounded by apple trees. It had a cellar where we kept potatoes, a small barn and a fenced pasture where we kept our one horse and few cows, and an outhouse where I first experimented with smoking a pipe. It was near the red brick consolidated school where my married sisters Wanda and Naomi had gone to high school, and where I was then in the fourth grade.

One day when Daddy was home I was busy with other thoughts, but a strange conversation between my parents, standing face to face on the linoleum-covered floor of the living room, caught my attention and cut a place into my memory.

"All right, if you're through with me, I'm through with you," Mama said, with finality. I didn't until much later connect the words with the events that shortly followed.

It was getting close to Christmas. I had already found a shiny metal toy dump truck and other toys hidden in the closet, but hadn't let on that I knew about them. Mama, without preliminaries, opened the closet door, took out our gifts and gave them to my sister Rose and me. Gordon, our baby brother, was too young to understand.

"We won't have any Christmas," Mama said, "so here are your presents early." I was shocked. It didn't seem right somehow. It was like getting to eat your dessert first and then not enjoying the meal.

Daddy loaded our household goods onto a trailer, moved us to an even smaller, more remote Arkansas town, Pyatt, and rented a four-room house for four dollars a month. He bought himself a 1939 Plymouth and headed for California, leaving Mama with a few chickens, a five-dollar bill, and us three little kids.

Pyatt was even more isolated than Bergman. At least Bergman had a railroad and a paved highway. In Pyatt it was an event for the kids to run and see when a car passed through. On a very busy day eight cars would pass through on the dirt road that was also the main street. Few would stop at the only filling station and buy gasoline, pumped by hand through a glass measuring tank atop the gasoline pump.

Daddy was gone three months. We could buy milk for a dime a gallon, and we could buy a wagon load of wood for a dollar, if we had a dollar. Sometimes that winter we burned bits of coal I had gathered from along the railroad. Some of the Jehovah's Witnesses from Harrison brought food. On one occasion they brought some wheat. Mama boiled it; we put milk and sugar on it and ate it as cereal.

Mama had come a long way from her marriage to a "rich man" twenty-one years before. He had just come back from France after World War I; he had had an oil well and a Cadillac. A short time after they met, they fell in love and married. His fortune had gradually dwindled until now he owned only a small acreage in Arkansas and a new car, high perhaps for Depression standards, but like many other men of that day, he had abandoned his family. "That d___ religion" had been the final excuse for the break, but the marriage was on the rocks long before the lady with the phonograph and book satchel showed up.

It was at Pyatt that I first saw people pray before a meal. I was invited to supper at a playmate's home. The entire family sat down at an oilcloth-covered table around a simple, but plentiful meal. I noticed that they all sat with hands in their laps, and looked expectantly at the father. Dressed in blue denim work clothes, his tanned face was lined by daily hours of labor in the sun. He surveyed his family, then bowed his head. They all bowed their heads, so I did too. The man began to talk to God.

Perhaps I had heard people pray before, and I was just now big enough to understand it, but this is the first time I can remember hearing anyone pray. The man was strong. His family looked up to him, respected him. He talked to God like he knew Him, but with deep reverence. I felt as if I had, for the very first time in my life, come into the very presence of God. Hearing the prayer, eating the food that had been blessed, was the most religious experience of my young life.

My mother had been spiritually destitute. Her children had visited the Oregon Flats Baptist Church, but in her time of religious crisis, that church had not visited her. She had visited the Bergman Methodist Church, but in her time of need she was not visited by that church. Someone else, carrying a phonograph and book satchel, had walked up that dirt road to fill the void in Mama's heart.

In Pyatt we were physically destitute. There were Christians around who loved God, but it was the Witnesses from Harrison that brought the wheat.

The Witnesses came regularly and had "Bible studies," using the *Watchtower* magazines and the Watchtower books.

The Witnesses make heavy use of the words "Bible study." But in reality they study *The Watchtower* magazine and Watchtower books. In years past many people have read only the Bible and decided that the right church for them was Baptist, Methodist, Presbyterian, interdenominational, Catholic, and many others. But none have ever read just the Bible and decided that the right church was the Jehovah's Witnesses.

The only way a person can become a Jehovah's Witness is to be indoctrinated *by* Jehovah's Witnesses. And the only way a person can remain a Witness is for him to consume a steady diet of the Society's doctrines. Russell recognized that fact and wrote about it: "Furthermore, not only do we find that people cannot see the divine plan in studying the Bible by itself, but we see, also, that if anyone lays the Scripture Studies aside, even after he has used them, after he has become familiar with them, after he has read them for ten years—if he then lays them aside and ignores them and goes to the Bible alone, though he has understood his Bible for ten years, our experience shows that within two years he goes into darkness. On the other hand, if he had merely read the Scripture Studies with their references and had not read a page of the Bible as such, he would be in the light at the end of two years, because he would have the light of the Scriptures" (*The Watch Tower,* Sept. 15, 1910, page 298).

In practice then and today, the Witnesses' Bible study in a prospect's home involves studying a *Watchtower* magazine or a Watchtower-published book, and looking up the scripture references, which the Witness explains.

Mama was receptive to the doctrine that organized religion had failed. It had certainly failed her. It had failed to straighten out the evils of the world. It had failed in her heart. All other religions were lumped into the same mold and labeled, "Organized Religion," and "Failed!" An important part of her indoctrination was to, without consideration, disbelieve anything *Organized Religion* claimed. After all, *Organized Religion* had failed. She did not realize that she was being brainwashed into the most organized religion on the face of the earth, to join the ranks of the most disciplined and regimented religious followers.

One of Judge Rutherford's favorite expressions was "Religion is a snare and a racket." He denied that the Watchtower Society was a religion. The contradiction that the most religious people in the world did not *practice* religion, years later became an embarrassment to the Society and additional *New Light* made them decide that it *was* a religion after all. The disciplined followers promptly erased from their minds the catchphrase, *Religion is a snare and a racket.*

To be a Jehovah's Witness, Mama had to learn to develop compartmentalized thinking. She learned to think about only one doctrine at a time, and not let the thoughts be influenced by contradictions from other Watchtower doctrines. For example, using the word "congregation" or "Ecclesia," instead of "church," and ignoring the fact that they meant the same thing. Using a word in Greek or Hebrew rather than the vernacular is a favorite method of the Watchtower Society in utilizing this compartmentalized thinking, as we will see later. Years later, after the *New Light* showed that theirs was a religion, they also received *New Light* that a congregation or assembly was a church.

All the time Daddy was gone the Witnesses came to Pyatt with regularity, and Mama became more and more indoctrinated. She wrote to Uncle Al, who was living in Augusta, Kansas, and was a leader in the Wichita, Kansas, Company of Jehovah's Witnesses. (In those days their Congregations were called "Companies.")

One bright afternoon we saw a shiny gray 1939 Plymouth drive in. The back seat of the car was loaded with sacks and boxes of groceries. Daddy was all smiles. He hugged us, and told us how glad he was to see us. Mama was cool.

He gave Rose and me his violin and a sack of foreign coins, which became our prized possessions. He stayed a few days and left again for California. World War II was approaching. People were flocking from Arkansas to California to work in the aircraft factories. Daddy was making money taking them there in his car.

As he drove away, we stood on the front porch and watched. As we lost sight of the car, Mama said half to herself, "He's going to be surprised when he comes back and we're gone."

A few days later, a gray 1936 Terraplane, pulling a trailer, drove up, and out of the car came the tallest man I had ever seen. Wearing a white shirt and tie, he had white hair, combed straight back, and wore sparkling clean rimless glasses. He looked scholarly. In a deep voice he called Mama "Gracie."

It was Uncle Al. With him was his son-in-law, George Procter, a soft-spoken and gentle man who walked with a pronounced limp; one leg was quite shorter than the other due to an old injury.

Uncle Al took charge. He had an auction sale on our front porch, and sold everything we couldn't pack on the trailer. Soon our family was squeezed into the back seat of the Terraplane and we were on the road to the big city.

2
In "The Truth"

In Augusta, Kansas, we spent a few days in Uncle Al's apartment behind his barber and beauty shop on the second floor of a downtown business building. It smelled like over-chlorinated city water: strange. It had no yard and no trees, but it did have electric lights and an indoor toilet, and a refrigerator that ran on natural gas.

I was so fascinated by the pull switch on an electric light that I stood on a chair and pulled it, turning the light on and off about a hundred times. Uncle Al came in and lectured me on waste. It cost two or three cents every time I pulled that string, he said. I was humiliated and ashamed, and longed for familiar surroundings.

Aunt Alta was just as sweet and kind as Uncle Al was overbearing and brusque. She was soft and fat, ate the pie but left the crust, and was tolerant of ignorant kids.

Al complained a lot, talking about his health, and fatigue, and gave himself liver extract injections in the thigh every day. If he didn't he would die, he said.

Uncle Al was treated with reverence by the other Witnesses. He was one of "The Elect." Mama explained to me that *The Elect* were those who would go to heaven when they died. There were only a *hundred and forty-four thousand* of them altogether, she said, and they included Uncle Al, and leaders of the Watchtower Society.

"How do you know you are of *The Elect?*" I asked.

"I just know," he said, and closed the subject.

Uncle Al believed that he was sure to go to heaven

when he died, but that it would be impossible for the great mass of people. When he spoke, and he was often the principal speaker at meetings, the Witnesses listened. And when the Society spoke, he listened.

What a disciplined Witness fears more than anything else is ostracism by his peers. To disagree with the Society on anything means being "disfellowshipped," being called an "evil servant," and losing one's eternal life. Therefore, when the Society comes out with *New Light*, every Witness accepts it.

They ridicule the Pope in Rome, and deplore the Catholic's obedience to him. But the Witnesses have no individual thought, no personal freedom; like the good Catholic who believes that when the Pope speaks ex cathedra it is the voice of the personal vicar of Christ on earth, so do the Witnesses believe the pronouncements of the Society are those of Jehovah God Himself.

Watchtower publications often picture caricatures of the Catholic hierarchy, dressed in long, lace dresses. The Society hierarchy doesn't wear long lace dresses, but its function is the same as the Catholic Hierarchy, except it is *less* tolerant of diverse opinion.

From Augusta we moved to Wichita and stayed a few weeks with Al's daughter, Wilda Procter and her husband George. They had lost a 14-year-old son whom they called "Little George," in a bicycle accident. Wilda had a worn, wooden chest of the boy's belongings which she frequently took out and ritualistically displayed while weeping. She spoke of the resurrection, and her hope of seeing Little George again. Wilda's husband George's 16-year-old daughter by a previous marriage, Marie, lived with them. She was constantly reminded of how stupid and clumsy she was, and was so cowed that she jumped every time anyone spoke or moved.

Wilda, George, and Marie were all "in *The Truth,*" and Mama was in *The Truth* because they were Jehovah's Witnesses. A neighbor across the street, Ray Alexander, who had been in *The Truth* a long time, became acquainted with us, and was a help in many ways to the newly displaced grass widow and her three children.

Ray owned twelve acres of land on North Arkansas Avenue in Wichita and planned to build a "trailer park" there for the Witnesses. Many Witnesses lived in travel trailers and spent most of their time going door to door placing Watchtower publications. They were discouraged from forming any permanent attachments because "Armageddon could come any day."

The Wichita Kingdom Hall was upstairs at Second and Main Streets, in an area of beer joints, sleazy hotels, and cheap upstairs apartments. Boards on the long, wide staircase creaked, and the higher one went the more pronounced was the odor of old plaster, dust and old stained woodwork. Upstairs was the Hall, a large open room with a high ceiling. It seated more than 200 on folding chairs. In the summer heat electric fans passed the heavy, hot air back and forth to be breathed again and again, supplemented by hand fans furnished by a local funeral home. The wood floor creaked as small groups of standing Witnesses visited with one another before the meeting. They called each other "brother" and "sister," and seemed to enjoy a family relationship.

On the left as we entered the Hall was a small room separated by half partitions with windows like a country post office. Behind these the various "servants" or officials worked. For example, the "book servant" had a window. He sold books to the Witnesses for resale; and there was another for the "territory servant," who issued small maps glued to the back of cards, and made a record of who worked door-to-door in each *territory*.

When a Witness checked out a *territory* to be worked, he had on the cards a record of previous work that had been done there. A line on the card for each home indicated when that home was last visited, if the Witness talked to a man or a woman, what kind of literature had been left, and what kind of reception had been given. If the householder was completely unreceptive or rude, the word "goat" was written there to warn the next Witness.

This was an allusion to Matthew 25:31-33: "When the Son of man shall come in his glory, and all the holy angels with him, then shall he sit upon the throne of his glory; And before him shall be gathered all nations: and he shall separate them one from another, as a shepherd divideth his sheep from the goats: And he shall set the sheep on his right hand, but the goats on the left."

Each Witness filled out a report slip showing how much time he had spent "in witness work" during the past week. All regulars were called "publishers" and in order to maintain that standing, they had to fill out the report regularly.

At the Kingdom Hall, Mama was warmly welcomed. Uncle Al was regarded as a deliverer. A collection was taken up, and Mama was presented with eighty-five dollars. On the way home, she wept.

For a woman who knew nothing about business, and who had not even managed her own affairs, Mama turned into an imaginative business woman. She rented an old two-story frame house for sixteen dollars a month. Its paint had long since faded, and it was surrounded by a rusty wire fence, and thick, untrimmed shrubbery. The backyard had tall cottonwood trees and an ancient outhouse with a flush toilet whose water roared down from an overhead tank through the bowl and directly into the sewer.

Inside plumbing had been added long after the house had been built.

On Broadway, the busiest street in the city and a major U.S. highway, our house and the house next door stood alone, the last residential holdouts in a business district. Mama divided the house into apartments and rented them.

We never again received charity, but we were on more of an austerity program than we had been even in Pyatt. We bought day-old bread for six cents a loaf, and were allowed one slice each at a meal. We had enough, but the idea of such strict rationing was unsettling. The Nomar Theater, a block and a half away, had Saturday matinees for kids, admission nine cents. Occasionally we got to go, but usually we got our own money by picking up pop bottles and selling them for two cents each.

An elderly man, Mr. Hill, who had a small watch repair shop in the neighborhood was in *The Truth* and therefore trustworthy. A lonely widower, he occasionally bought groceries for the family and came over for a home-cooked meal. I had not seen anyone like Mr. Hill before. Unlike the rough tobacco-chewing Arkansas farmers in bib overalls, he always wore a white shirt, was pale, bald, slight, stooped, and weak. (I had not realized that he was then near the end of his life. He died just a few years later.)

Kind Mr. Hill fit the description of those who would never attain eternal life, according to the Watchtower preaching. He never went out witnessing. He rarely came to the Hall. He was a nominal member of the Witnesses, but just didn't measure up by enduring *faithfully to the end.* No one said that about him personally. But we who listened to the talks at the Hall believed it, and privately wondered about ourselves and each other.

We had a regular ride to the Hall with Ray Alexander in his black 1932 Pontiac. He was a forty-five-year-old bachelor, with coarse thick black hair, graying at the temples. Painfully shy, he seemed to almost apologize for being present, but he was strong in what he believed and he believed in Jehovah and the Society. He lived with his mother at the front of his twelve-acre tract. Rose, Gordon, and I loved Ray from the start.

After we were in Wichita about a year, Daddy came with divorce papers for Mama to sign because he wanted to remarry. He took back the violin and old coins he had given us in Arkansas, and gave Rose and me each a silver dollar. Our hearts were broken to lose those small symbols of our father's love, but we didn't show it. We went to town and each bought a pair of cheap roller skates which, on the rough sidewalks, wore out in a few days. The violin and old coins, tokens of our father's love, had been exchanged for emptiness.

We went to school with instructions not to salute the flag, and were taught to memorize the scripture: "Thou shalt have no other gods before me. Thou shalt not make unto thee any graven image, or any likeness of any thing that is in heaven above, or that is in the earth beneath, or that is in the water under the earth. Thou shalt not bow down thyself to them, nor serve them . . ." (Exodus 20:3-5).

That's what the Bible said. And Mama said it included flags, so we refused to salute the flag. We heard reports of other Witness kids that were persecuted for not saluting the flag. "Persecuted" is a key word in the Witness vocabulary. Any time a Witness is *persecuted* it authenticates him and he is better regarded by his peers.

Most people were preoccupied with the war then going on in Europe and the Pacific. With the Witnesses the expectation was for the "New World" coming soon when, following the Battle of Armageddon, they would have eternal life on a perfect earth.

In 1942 in a book entitled *The New World* Rutherford said, "... THE NEW WORLD IS AT THE
DOORS ... The Time is short."

I did not realize anything was up when Ray started
building us a cement block house at the rear of his
trailer park acreage. Shortly after we moved in,
Mama went away for two weeks (we assumed she
was out witnessing) and after she came back, she and
Ray gathered us around them and announced that
they had been secretly married several weeks before.

Suddenly I didn't like Ray anymore. I couldn't explain it, and didn't try to analyze the whys of my feel-
ings. A big 12-year-old boy, who hardly ever cried
even when hurt, that night cried himself to sleep. We
were constantly taught that Jehovah and the
witness work were to come before anything and
everything, including parents and children. But I
couldn't help feeling betrayed and excluded. I
wouldn't allow myself to think a bad thought about
Mama, so I took it all out on Ray.

Ray tried to be a father to Rose and me, but we rejected him. Gordon was tickled with the arrange-
ment, but when he tried to call Ray "Daddy," we
made fun of him and he stopped. Ray expected us to
act like grownups, and when we failed he was hard on
us, and we were harder on him.

From the time in Arkansas when our Christmas
gifts were given early, we never observed Christmas.
We were told that it was a pagan holiday, as were all
holidays. I always dreaded Christmas because the
anticipation and joy the other children felt was so
conspicuously absent in our home, and because of the
embarrassment that always followed in school when
the teacher asked everyone to tell the class what they
got for Christmas. My married sisters, Wanda and
Naomi, kept it from being a complete disaster,
because each year they sent a box of gifts for the
family whether we believed in it or not. In class when

our turn came, my sister Rose and I would tell about the pair of socks or other small gifts we had received from our older sisters.

I often remembered happier days in Arkansas when Daddy would go out into the woods and cut a Christmas tree, usually a cedar which would reach to the ceiling. On Christmas Eve after we had gone to bed he and Mama would decorate it and put the presents around it. They told us Santa Claus did it, but we knew better, and just went along with them to humor them. After we became Witnesses, the joyful season became the barren season.

Neither did we observe birthdays. When we were small children, Mama baked two cakes in May, one for Rose and one for me, for Rose's birthday. She baked two more for us in August for my birthday. But after we were in *The Truth* all that stopped.

The basis for the Witnesses not celebrating Christmas is not from Scripture, but because of the pagan origins of many Christmas traditions. To reject commemoration and celebration of the incarnation of Christ because some ancient pagans had a celebration during the same season is nonsense. We could pick any season and determine that the pagans had a celebration then. Because pagans used a tree decorated with gold and silver in some of their rites is no more reason to shun use of a Christmas tree than it is to cut down all trees in our yards because ancient pagans worshiped trees. Christmas is a wonderful opportunity to call the attention of a lost world to the incarnation of the Messiah, God in the flesh, Who came to redeem us from our sins.

One of the high points of my childhood was when Ray took us to the International Convention of Jehovah's Witnesses at the World's Fairgrounds in St. Louis. A new book entitled *Children* was introduced, and the Society president, Nathan H. Knorr, made an address directed especially to the children. Hundreds of children responded; they and many adult converts were baptized in a swimming pool nearby.

The thousands attending had a common bond in the sincere conviction that Armageddon would come within months. I was becoming spiritually sensitive. I had previously tried hard to live a sinless life, and to work faithfully in the Witness work and thereby gain eternal life, but I had failed. I would do fine for awhile, then I would think bad thoughts; I would have an opportunity to witness to someone and wouldn't do it; I would fail to study the *Watchtower*; or I wouldn't want to go to the Hall. (I would go anyway, but my attitude was wrong.) I realized that I was a sinner, and that my sin was against Jehovah God. At the St. Louis Convention I made a vow to myself that I would never sin again in thought, word, or deed, by commission or omission, in order to be in a right standing with God, and to gain eternal life.

One day in St. Louis, Mama dressed me in a spotless white linen suit. There was a period that afternoon when there was nothing to do at the convention, so we visited the St. Louis Zoo. A great crowd gathered around a monkey cage where a large chimpanzee was playing with a water hose. I worked my way toward the front of the crowd so I could see. When I was in the center of the crowd, the ape turned the hose on the crowd. They turned and ran, knocking me down into the mud.

I had the same experience with a sinless life that I had with the white linen suit; it was crumpled and smeared with mud. I tried and tried, but failed and failed. I began to think there was something peculiar about me. The other Witness kids didn't seem to be having the trouble with conscience that I had. I thought perhaps they were succeeding where I was failing.

3
"Enduring Faithfully to the End"

The Society had a program called the "Theocratic Ministry," in which every male was encouraged to enroll. I enrolled at the age of eleven, was taught to prepare and deliver "talks," and with fear and trembling soon made my first well-rehearsed six-minute talk to an audience of about two hundred Witnesses at the Hall.

During my years as a Witness, at least once, and sometimes two or three times a week, we would go to downtown Wichita street corners to "put out" the *Watchtower*. We carried the magazines in canvas shoulder bags on which were emblazoned in red letters, "Watchtower." We were instructed to hold up a copy of *The Watchtower* magazine and say "Watchtower," to each passerby, and to add some phrase such as "Announcing Jehovah's Kingdom."

World War II was going on and the Witnesses were well-known for their refusal to salute the flag and serve in the Armed Forces. Oftentimes I heard people mutter, "If you don't like this country, why don't you leave ... Germans ... spies ..." or "Japs." This did not deter us. We had been warned to expect *persecution* from "the World."

In our sixth grade classroom, it was customary every morning for the children to pledge allegiance to the flag; my sister and I would stand mute, our hands to our sides. In my heart I doubted that the scripture forbidding idolatry applied to saluting the flag, but I tried not to think about it. I loved my country, and wanted to be a loyal American. The accusations on the streets when I was putting out the *Watchtower*, the questioning glances from my classmates during the pledge of allegiance, and the patronizing "All right" from the unconvinced teacher after I had explained the "scriptural basis" for not saluting the flag, combined with the doubt already in my heart and caused continual conflict within me.

On one occasion, six boys tried to force me to salute the flag. It was a warm afternoon, and I was walking to a neighborhood gasoline station-grocery store, where kids hung out to drink soda pop and gossip. The boys surrounded me on the gravel driveway, and told me I was going to salute the flag. I told them I was not.

"I respect the flag, and what it stands for, but I will not salute it, because it would be bowing down to a graven image, which is against the Scripture . . ." The boys didn't let me finish my often-recited explanation, but cursed me and my parentage, and with fists and feet, beat me to the ground. They held me there, while one boy held up a tiny, crumpled American flag, and ordered, "Now, salute it!"

I refused, and the fists and feet beat my face down into the driveway until sand and gravel were in my mouth and sand was in my eyes. My resolve was not to submit to their force even if they killed me (which for a time I thought they might). They finally gave up and left me. Skinned from head to toe from the mauling on the gravel, I felt hatred for the young thugs, but I also felt heartsick that such conflict had to exist, especially when deep down, I felt it was unnecessary.

The heroes of the JW's in those days were the young men who refused to be drafted into the Armed Forces. They refused to submit to induction, and were put on trial as draft evaders. They were offered conscientious objectors' status, but refused it, saying that they were "ordained ministers of the Gospel," and as such should be exempted. This claim was not recognized, because all Witnesses claimed to be ordained ministers, ordained by Jehovah God Himself.

I remember well one trial I attended. The defendant was good-looking, clean cut, and expressed himself well. He had not asked for a jury trial; the judge called the young man forward to the bench and asked him if he did not love his country, and if he would not reconsider, and do his part to protect his community and family. The defendant continued to refuse, much to the admiration of the Witnesses present.

The young man was given a five-year sentence in Federal prison. I heard a spectator remark, "It takes more guts to do that than to go to the Army."

One of my best friend's older brothers was sacrificed to the penitentiary. The younger boys admired him. He was smart, had an almost new 1940 Ford, a good job, and a lovely wife. John (not his real name) was called by his draft board; true to his lifelong instructions, he refused to be inducted, and went to trial. The judge called him forward and pleaded with him not to ruin his life, and not to forsake his country in its time of need. John was moved by the judge's words, and changed his mind: he would go into the Army. In the courtroom the Witnesses were shocked. They pitied John's family for the disgrace he had brought upon it.

After several months in the Army, the conflict in John's own heart got the best of him, and he refused to salute an officer on the grounds of "idolatry." When he was called on the carpet for the violation of military courtesy, he refused to serve as a soldier any longer.

In Leavenworth, Kansas, Federal Penitentiary, John was again a hero to the Witnesses, but not to himself. His friends were fighting and dying on foreign fields; he had been labeled a "dishonor," and locked up. It was too much for him; he cracked.

After being confined for about two years, most of the time in mental wards, John was released to his parents. His wife had long since divorced him. He had grown a beard, and his eyes had taken on a wild, glazed look as if he didn't really see people. To my knowledge, John never recovered. As far as I know the conflicts are still there; like a typewriter with its keys jammed, his mind just locked up and refused to function.

When asked why these young men would not serve their country, and I was asked often, I would quote the scripture: "My kingdom is not of this world: if my kingdom were of this world, then would my servants fight" (John 18:36). I had not considered this answer but was programmed to quote it in answer to that particular question. But I secretly wondered about it, especially in view of the attitude of Jesus toward soldiers. Jesus had had contact with soldiers and He never told them to desert; He never told them to refuse to salute their officers. He never told anyone to refuse military service (Matthew 8:9-10).

John the Baptist likewise did not encourage soldiers to become rebellious or discourteous, but did the opposite in telling them to be honest in the discharge of their duty and to be content with their wages (Luke 3:14). Jesus and John had had plenty of opportunity to make such statements as the Witnesses now made, but had not done so.

The Apostle Paul had likened Christians to soldiers, and likewise had expressed no indications that Christians were to refuse to serve their countries, but rather cautioned them to be obedient to civil authority. I tried not to think about these things; I tried to practice the necessary compartmentalized thinking, but these truths kept getting over the partitions and caused conscious conflicts.

Then I did something that was the beginning-of-the-end of my discipline as a Witness: I read the scripture in context. Jesus was standing in the judgment hall before the Roman Governor Pontius Pilate, who asked, "Art thou the King of the Jews? . . . Thine own nation and the chief priests have delivered thee unto me: what hast thou done?" Pilate was asking why, if Jesus were King of the Jews, His own people would deliver Him up to be judged, and why His supporters did not defend Him to keep Him from being taken to be put to death.

Jesus answered, "My kingdom is not of this world: if my kingdom were of this world, then would my servants fight, that I should not be delivered to the Jews: but now is my kingdom not from hence." (The Witnesses had memorized only the first half of the verse.)

To be intellectually honest, I had to admit that the use of this scripture had been wrong. Jesus was not talking about military service. He had come into the world to die for our sins, not to set up an earthly kingdom at that time. My use of the scripture had been out of context. By cutting off Jesus' statement in the middle of a sentence the Society had been using it dishonestly.

But a Witness cannot disagree with the Society on any point of doctrine. If I had announced to the Witnesses my discovery and told them that I believed it was permissible for a Christian to serve in the Armed Forces, I would have been *disfellowshipped*, even though I accepted all the other Watchtower doctrines. There is no room for any diverse opinion in *The Truth*. All Scripture must be interpreted the same way that the Watchtower Society interprets it.

I then examined more closely Exodus 20:3-5, "Thou shalt have no other gods before me. Thou shalt not make unto thee any graven image, or any likeness of any thing that is in heaven above, or that is in the earth beneath, or that is in the water under the earth. Thou shalt not bow down thyself to them, nor serve them."

Now that one partition in my compartmentalized thinking had begun to break down, I objectively examined this scripture. I could not see how it could apply to the flag. If it applied to a flag, it would also apply to making a snapshot, a painting, or a map.

The Witnesses thought these things were all right, but they didn't allow the flag doctrine to get into that "compartment." I could love my mother without worshiping her. I could have a picture of my mother without worshiping it. I could love my country without worshiping it; and I was becoming convinced I could salute the flag, which stood for America, without worshiping it.

But I didn't salute the flag. I kept these new convictions a secret. I still went to the Hall. I gradually quit going out in the Witness work, which was apparent—the weekly reports every active "publisher" is required to make reflected my lack of work.

I wondered about *enduring faithfully to the end,* which was a great source of anxiety to me, and to other Witnesses. As I read my Bible, I saw in the New Testament people who heard the preaching of Jesus or the disciples, and became converted, and were joyfully baptized. It just wasn't the same picture I saw in the Witnesses. Those in the New Testament who became Christians seemed like people who were released from bondage; people who became Witnesses seemed like those who went into bondage.

My mother would often ask me, "Have you just quit?" I would give a lame excuse for my non-performance as a Witness. I was afraid to tell her about my discoveries, because I knew how she feared ostracism. Sometimes Mama would weep and say, "I'm afraid I won't get life (the resurrection) because

I have failed in raising my children." (My sister Rose had quit doing Witness work before I did.) I dared not express any doubts about the Watchtower doctrines because I did not want to hurt my mother.

No person ever sat down and told me how wrong these doctrines were, but one individual did help to solidify my thinking, and he was a Witness, who did it unintentionally. This man, who I will call Mr. Miller, owned more than 2,000 acres of fine Western Kansas wheat land. My family had gotten acquainted with him at the Hall, and he had asked if I could come to his farm and work the summer. Thirteen was too young, my mother said, but Mr. Miller promised that he would treat me as his own son, and that it would be a "great experience" for me. I wanted to go more than anything. Finally she relented.

Mr. Miller lived in a beautiful home on the prairie surrounded by a sea of the "amber waves of grain." The home had several bedrooms, but I was told to sleep on a cot in the basement. Mr. Miller had a wife, who was an invalid, and was confined most of the time to her room. I saw him "making sport" with the cook, a woman some 20 years younger than himself, and I also guessed why they both came out of the same bedroom, and why I, and the other hired hand, slept in the basement.

During part of the summer, it was my job to take more than thirty head of cattle, including a Hereford bull, to a pasture a couple of miles from the house each morning and watch after them while they grazed. Mr. Miller had only one horse, but it was so wild, and I was so inexperienced, I couldn't handle it. The nearest neighbor, who lived about two miles away, had several horses, one of which was a well-trained cow pony that he allowed me to use much of the time. As long as I was on horseback I enjoyed taking care of the cattle, but hated to have to do it afoot. I didn't like being two miles from the nearest fence, and ten miles from the nearest tree in the presence of an ill-tempered bull.

I wondered why kind people like these neighbors were without hope of eternal life while Mr. Miller, who was unkind and exceedingly selfish, could look forward to the resurrection. It seemed very confusing.

On one of the days when I was afoot, the bull didn't begin grazing like the other cattle when we arrived in the pasture, but stood with his front feet apart, and his head down looking at me. I pretended to ignore him, but kept watch out of the corner of my eye. Then he started to blow through his nostrils, his eyes still affixed to my vulnerable form. I had heard that in a situation like that the best thing to do is to ignore the animal, and I was trying my best, but my strongest impulse was to run, but where, and to what?

I was already tired from the walk out to the pasture and sprints after strays. If I started to run, he would surely chase, in the mood he was in, and it would be just a matter of time before I would be overtaken. I could just imagine one of his horns piercing the small of my back as he overtook me!

Then he began to snort and to walk toward me, pawing the ground, sending clumps of grass, sandy loam and dust flying behind him. I remembered something else I had heard: "Show no fear." (I couldn't remember where I had heard that stuff, but at the moment it was all I had.) I turned and faced the bull. Ten feet away, he stopped his advance, but continued to paw the ground and snort.

I did my best to show no fear, but inside I was trembling and about to panic. Then a miracle happened. In the midst of hundreds of acres of nothing but dirt and grass, at my feet I saw a one-by-six inch pine board about five feet long. Weathered and gray, it had been lying there a long time. God only knows how it got there, but there it was. I then decided to "show no fear" in the most dramatic way possible, though it might be the last act of my life. I picked up the board, walked briskly to the bull, and hit him between the eyes as hard as I could and hollered at him at the top of my voice. The startled bull turned and trotted away.

I had been face to face with death. I still shook inside, but I realized that some power outside myself had kept me from getting killed.

On another occasion, Mr. Miller stationed me at the top of the huge grain bins in his private grain elevator. I was to stand on a two-by-twelve inch plank which had been laid from one bin to the other, parallel to a chute through which wheat was pouring into one of the bins. Forty feet below me was the grain elevator floor where trucks passed through, and dumped their grain down through a grillwork of two-inch steel pipes. Looking straight down from the plank on which I stood, I could imagine how uncomfortable it might be to fall, and land on those pipes.

My job was to walk along the plank, and with a small board in my hands, free any clumps of grain that stopped up the grain chute. Occasionally a clump would stop the flow, but before I could break up the clump with my board, the chute would overflow, and spill grain over me, and over the plank on which I stood. After a few hours, it became routine and I became accustomed to walking on the plank to get to the troublesome clumps.

Suddenly my feet slipped on the wheat-covered plank, and in an instant I was falling. Instinctively I sucked in my breath and caught the plank with my hands as I fell. Grasping the far edge of the plank, my weight on my forearms caused the kernels of grain to press between the plank and my flesh, and my legs dangled in space. Then the far edge of the plank I held began to tip up and toward me. If it tipped over, I would lose my hold, and fall. This time

I was not panicky, but calmly thought it was the end of my life.

With all the strength I could bring to bear, I pushed forward until the board went down from its forty-five degree angle, and lay flat again in its place. I then was able to throw a leg over the board and carefully, so it would not tip again, climb back up. This was the second time I had almost been killed. Why had I been spared again?

Mr. Miller expected me to work harder than I had expected to work, so I decided to go home in the middle of the summer. He refused permission, and when I announced that I would walk to town and hitchhike home, he threatened me with a board, and I decided to stay.

The man could afford any kind of food, but Mr. Miller had lots of chickens, so we lived on eggs. Many times we had eggs three times a day. We had fried eggs, boiled eggs, scrambled eggs, every variety of eggs. After that experience I didn't eat an egg for a year.

I really wasn't worth much as a farm hand. The going pay for adult workers was $12 a day, but I knew I wouldn't get near that, and rightly so. At the end of the summer, Mr. Miller sat me down and told me what a sorry hand I had been, and figured at the most, I was worth a dollar a day to him. Then he deducted my food and lodging, leaving $30 for three months work, less than what other hands got for three days.

On the way back to Wichita on the bus, I counted up the score against "good Witness" Mr. Miller: liar, adulterer, greedy lover of money, slave driver, and thief. He was certainly not representative of the Witnesses, but he did prove that they weren't all upright.

Other things had happened during those three months. I had turned fourteen; I had grown three inches (which speaks well for the egg diet), and my voice was changing. Most of the time I sounded like a man, but sometimes I sounded like a boy, and sometimes I sounded like Tarzan.

I had never been allowed to fight. If someone attacked me, I was never to strike back. If I came home with a bloody nose, or a swollen lip, I got into trouble for fighting. I didn't like to fight anyway, but sometimes it was unavoidable. A neighbor boy whom we called "B.E.," and who was not a Witness, about a head shorter than I was, had been bullying me before I had gone off to Mr. Milller's, because he knew I was not allowed to fight. When I got back home I was ready to renounce the whole Watchtower doctrine, especially the pacifism, but I didn't do it; I still feared hurting my mother. Instead, I beat the tar out of B.E.

I did not know what doctrine was right, but I knew much of the Watchtower doctrine was wrong, yet I was still identified as a Witness. I felt like a hypocrite. But I was so programmed that if any person asked me why Jehovah's Witnesses wouldn't serve in the Armed Forces, "My Kingdom is not of this world, etc.," would come out of my mouth as if I were a tape recorder.

4
A Void in My Heart

By the time I was fifteen, I was big enough to pass the adult test. I could walk into a beer joint by myself, put my foot on the brass rail and order a beer, which would be served without my age being questioned.

Shortly before I left home, my sister and I, alone at home, bought six bottles of beer and sat down on the living room floor to drink them. We had drunk a half bottle apiece when my mother arrived unexpectedly. Carrying a sack of groceries, she walked through the room, and seeing the beer bottles, a shocked expression came over her face.

"You kids shouldn't be doing that," she said, and walked by us and into the kitchen. I expected at least to be killed, but no more was said. We both considered that lack of reaction a license.

I had a heavy relationship with a girl who moved from Wichita, Kansas, to Enid, Oklahoma. I had been working the summer as an oilfield roughneck and had a pocketful of money, so I went with her. For a year I had been ready to leave the religious discipline and my mother and stepfather. The family discipline and religious discipline were hopelessly mixed together in my mind. The girlfriend's departure, together with having the financial means, were enough to finalize my decision to leave home.

A few months later, in Enid, Oklahoma, I lied about my age and joined the Army. I said nothing to my family, but as far as they were concerned I had just vanished. The break was complete. When I threw over the Watchtower discipline, I also threw over other common disciplines. As a result I got drunk often and got into trouble.

In the Army Air Corps, I missed my family, especially my little brother, Gordon, so on my first furlough, I went home for a visit. During the visit in Wichita, Ray invited me to go to Augusta, fifteen miles away, with him to visit Uncle Al. When we arrived in downtown Augusta, we parked near the two-story red brick building where Al lived on the second floor behind his barber and beauty shop. As we got out of the car, and Ray put a coin in the parking meter, we saw Al walking down the sidewalk toward us.

Ray greeted him, "Hello, Al."

I had always admired Uncle Al, and was glad to see him. I eagerly extended my hand, smiled, and said, "Hello, Uncle Al."

He surveyed my uniform, ignored my hand, and half turned toward Ray, and said, "Hello, Ray," and as if I were non-existent, he turned his back to me completely and began chatting with Ray.

I was to him "as one dead." There could be no communication with me. Al had not been ordered by the Society to do this; he had done it on his own. Twenty-five years later, Mama and Ray would be ordered by the Society to do the same thing, of which I will speak more later.

In the occasional contacts I had with my family they usually communicated to me the urgency of the situation: *Armageddon could come at any time.* This sense of urgency was kept in their hearts for decades. Nathan H. Knorr, who had taken over as president of the Society when Rutherford died in 1942, continued with Russell's and Rutherford's regular prophecies of Armageddon. In 1946 he said, "The disaster of Armageddon, greater than that which befell Sodom and Gomorrah, is at the door" (*Let God Be True,* page 194). In 1950 he said, "The march is on! Where? To the field of Armageddon for the 'war of the great day of God Almighty'!" (*This Means Everlasting Life*, page 311).

I was not yet seventeen when I was discharged from the Army (actually, my enlistment was canceled because I was underage).

I wandered from city to city, and state to state, searching for I knew not what.

In a small town in Illinois, while working in a sheet metal shop, I met a young man who, it turned out, was a lunatic. While I was six feet one inch tall, he was short, no more than five-foot two, with red hair and freckles. The only name I ever heard anyone call him was "Red." Red and I became friends quickly.

This was my first experience with a lunatic, and I didn't know that it was not safe to disagree. One day, while working in the shop, we got into what I thought was a friendly argument over something so inconsequential I can't remember what it was. I laughed at him for his illogical arguments, and dismissed the conversation, which it turned out, was an error in judgment on my part.

Red didn't smile or change expression in any way. He simply announced that he was going to get his knife and kill me. I thought it was dry humor, but learned a few minutes later that he meant it.

He came running toward me with a ten-inch homemade knife. I ran around behind a steel work table to get away from him. Red looked across the table, started to run around one way, and when he did, I went the opposite way; then he tried going the other direction, but I kept the table between us. Then he fell to his knees and quickly started crawling under the table toward me.

I picked up the first thing that was handy, a heavy piece of angle-iron about six feet long, and using it like a spear, put my full weight behind it and jabbed Red in the ribs. He was sufficiently disabled so that he quit trying to kill me that day, but as he painfully dragged himself out from under the table, in the same calm and expressionless tone of voice as before, said, "I'm going to kill you if it's the last thing I do."

It was then I decided life would be better with two or three states between Red and me. I had escaped death again.

Before our friendship abruptly ended in the sheet metal shop, Red had invited me to go to Mass with him. I had always heard that Catholicism was the scourge of the earth, the Whore of Revelation, and the chief false religion that was a *snare and a racket.* But since I had taken to investigating the Watchtower's claims, I decided to get some firsthand information.

Mass was strange to me, but fascinating: the gilded altar; the statues; the priest's colorful vestments; the altar boy, like a little lace-clad shadow, moving silently behind the priest; the tinkling bells; the congregation, on signal falling to their knees on the dark red, velvet-covered kneeling rail; the people, on signal looking contrite and pious, beating their breasts; and the hundreds of worshipers mumbling prayers in unison.

After Mass I asked the priest some questions. He invited me to attend a catechumen class that was just beginning. I could sit in with the new converts who were to learn how to be Catholics. I accepted.

I learned something about Catholicism. It was more like Jehovah's Witnesses than anything with which I had come in contact. They believed in the infallibility of the Pope; the JW's believed similarly in the infallibility of the Society. The Catholics over the years added such teachings as the Immaculate Conception of Mary; the Watchtower Society adds and subtracts doctrines continually, and are not questioned by disciplined followers who accept the *New Light.*

The Catholics took away from the Ten Commandments and pray before idols; the JW's added to the Ten Commandments and forbade to salute the flag. The Catholics added to the Law and forbade eating meat on Friday; the JW's added to the Old Testament Law and forbade to take blood transfusions. The Catholics believed that the only way one could be saved was to be an obedient Catholic; the JW's believed the only way one could be saved was to be an obedient Jehovah's Witness.

I went into the training with an open mind. I learned the catechism, the prayers, when to bow, and when to look pious and beat my breast during Mass. Around my neck, I wore a little Saint Christopher's medal, which the priest had given me. I studied my prayer book, said my rosary every night, went to Mass every Sunday, and never missed a catechumen class except the last one, which was to be my baptism and confirmation.

A void was still in my heart. Christianity had not soaked from the outside into my inner being.

I put several states between Red and me and stopped in Mitchell, South Dakota. Cliff Loon, a new and used car dealer, befriended me and gave me some fatherly advice: "Quit drinking, and go to church."

Cliff had been an alcoholic, but had been sober for ten years. He became a short-term father to me. I listened to him, not because of his logic, but because of his example, and because I admired and respected him, and he really cared. Cliff was probably convinced that not a word of his advice soaked in, but it did.

Cliff, his two brothers-in-law, and myself tried to sing Christian songs together as a quartet while Mrs. Loon played the piano. I'm sure my tenor was the weakest link, which doomed our success as a singing group. But there was success in another area. I learned that there was another religious life that was not all discipline and anxiety, but relaxed, friendly,

43

and peaceful; and the thoughts of a song, new to me, "Whispering Hope," were permanently etched in my memory (though I never learned all the tenor part). I learned too that people could have fun without drinking.

Cliff and his family were members of a Lutheran church. Several times he invited me to go to church, before I accepted. The pastor invited me to sing in the choir. My experience singing there brought the same satisfaction as had those sessions around the piano at Cliff's home.

One of my jobs in the service department of Cliff's car dealership was to go into a second floor showroom and start the engines on the approximately twenty shiny new cars there, one at a time, and let each one run a few minutes. On one cold morning, I decided to save time by starting them all, intending after the last one was started to go back and turn off the first ones. By the time the last one was started, the room was so full of exhaust smoke that I began to feel ill and lightheaded.

I started walking across the large showroom toward a window. My legs felt like jelly, and my eyesight began to blur. Half conscious, I staggered across the room and finally reached the old wooden window, encased in a solid masonry wall. It opened upward with my first feeble effort, and I lay over the window sill and half hung outside, expelling the carbon monoxide from my lungs and taking in great gasps of the ice-cold air, while the blue exhaust smoke billowed out the window above me.

Feeling recovered a few minutes later, I turned off the engines, running back to the window for air after turning off every few cars, and continued airing out the showroom. During all that time no other person entered the room. Had I passed out on my way to the window, I would have died there of stupidity.

This was the fourth time I had almost been killed.

It was as if some great force were intervening.

One evening Cliff picked me up at the one-room apartment I shared with two other young men, to take me to the church. On the way, the conversation turned to my life and what I was to do with it. I felt as if I were in the lap of luxury, riding in the soft deep seat of the Cadillac. And this was just one of several Cadillacs he could have driven. Cliff seemed to me to have it made financially, and more than that, he seemed to be happy. Yet he was not a greedy money-grubber like Mr. Miller. He was generous, yet thrifty, had a great sense of humor, and took time to be a temporary father to misplaced teenagers like Joe Hewitt. Cliff was concerned about my drinking.

He had seen me take off a shoe, revealing a hole in my sock.

"Why do you wear a sock like that?" he asked. I had several weeks before left my clothes in a Kansas hotel rather than pay the bill, and had arrived in town with nothing but the clothes on my back, and Cliff knew it. I had bought a few clothes, but still didn't have enough. I tried to reply, but didn't give a satisfactory answer to his question.

"You can't really afford a ten-cent glass of beer, can you?" Cliff asked.

"No. I guess not," I answered.

"Really now, if you can't afford to buy a new pair of socks, you surely can't afford a glass of beer, can you?" he pressed on.

"You're right," I said, reluctantly.

As long as Cliff knew me, I didn't let up in my drinking, and I showed him few signs of progress, but I never forgot the conversation. His reasoning stuck with me, and I have since shared it with many other boys and young men.

As we rode to church that evening, I was under conviction. There was something lacking in my life. I wished I could be like Cliff and have a fulfilled life.

His advice was: "Go to church. Keep on going to church, and you will find that you just get better and better. Gradually, your life will change."

I tried it, but my life didn't change. I was a sinner inside and I knew it. I soon lost the desire to go to church, and quit. Christianity still did not surround me and soak into my inner being.

The next stop on my wandering was a little prairie town twelve miles west of Mitchell, where I worked for a home repairman. I was there just a few days when I was invited to join the Volunteer Fire Department. I agreed to, but before any formalities of enlistment could be accomplished, the small town received an emergency call from Mitchell for assistance; the entire downtown section of the city was on fire. I jumped aboard the engine with the rest of the volunteers and we sped off toward a column of smoke rising from Mitchell.

We joined fire departments from twelve other cities and towns, and our group was assigned a station atop a one-story roof, to fight fire in an adjacent two-story drug store building. It was engulfed in flame. The roof had fallen into what looked like a burning hell.

Another man and myself, who didn't know any better, put ladders up against the brick wall that stood between us and the inferno, so we could play streams of water down into the roofless building and into the fire. Soon the other man's section of the wall crumbled, and he fell into the fire. I played water onto him while others dropped a ladder, and soon a scorched and coughing, but wiser, volunteer fireman emerged out of the smoke and fire. I decided a guy could get killed in that business, and learned from the other man's lesson. I moved my ladder from its precarious position.

Late in the afternoon as the army of firemen began to get the fires under control, another man and

46

myself were sent on an errand that took us down an alley behind an old stone hotel which had been destroyed by the fire. All the walls had collapsed inward except the rear wall, which still stood like a four-story high, stone fence, separating the alley from the debris of the burned out and collapsed hotel.

As we returned back through the alley behind the lone still-standing wall, we both felt an urgency to get out of the alley, and without a word to each other, both began running, careful not to trip over the three large fire hoses, taut with water pressure, which had been laid the length of the alley. As soon as we emerged from the alley, four stories of hand-cut stone and dusty mortar crashed down behind us in a heap, filling the alley. Had we not run, we would have been under that pile, crushed along with the fire hoses.

What caused us to suddenly run? Was it movement of the stones high above our heads, a shift in air currents as the top fell? Or was it something greater, much higher?

I didn't stay in one place very long. I was still searching. I was half sober one summer night walking down a skid row street in a Midwestern city when I passed the open door of a rescue mission. A kindly looking little old lady who had been standing in the door, reached out and took my arm.

"Come in here, son. I want to talk to you," came the motherly command; her grip on my arm tightened slightly, and she guided me into the mission, where we both sat on a pew. She smiled and produced a well-worn New Testament, and with a voice filled with concern began to tell me how Jesus loved me.

I had never heard such talk before. She said if I would trust in Jesus Christ as my Lord and Saviour that I would be saved.

I could see a reflection of God's love in this lady. I could see that she loved Jesus. She had a relationship with the Deity that I had not perceived in any other

47

person since the man in Pyatt, Arkansas, I had first heard pray at a meal. She begged me to accept Jesus as my Lord and Saviour.

"I wish I could have the faith you have," I said, and I meant it. She had peace in her heart. I had a void. But it didn't happen to me. I didn't believe as she did, though I wished it were possible for me to have her kind of faith. But I didn't want to pretend something was in my heart if it wasn't. I didn't want to go through some empty motion. So I walked back out into the street.

5
Filling the Void

My wanderings brought me back to Wichita.

I was still searching. In my heart the great void was still there, an empty place that had never been satisfactorily filled.

I had developed in my mind a "dream girl," unlike anyone I had ever met. She was tall, with long dark hair and big eyes. I felt that if I ever met her she would help fill that void.

One evening, while I was visiting long-time friends in Wichita, Marylou Covert came to visit the same friends. She exactly fit my dream girl specifications. She probably thought me odd because of the way I looked at her, and I immediately asked her to go out with me. After our mutual friends convinced her that I was really harmless, she accepted, and within hours after we left them I announced to her that I was going to marry her.

Less than a year later we were married.

Marylou and her parents were members of a small Pentecostal church, though they did not themselves practice speaking in tongues.

Mr. and Mrs. Covert were concerned that Marylou had married "a Jehovah's Witness."

She had not married a Jehovah's Witness any more than she had married a Catholic. As far as religion was concerned, I was a "nothing." I believed in God, and I was almost certain that the Bible was God's word, but beyond that was confusion. I had no confidence in any church or any *organized religion.*

Marylou's parents were worried that I would not be good for her, and they were right. But she was good for me. My life took on a new meaning and a new direction.

Shortly after I met my new father-in-law, Alvie Covert, he and I were in a car on an errand together. I was driving, and suggested that we stop at a pool hall and have a beer, and play a game of pool.

"No thanks. I don't drink," Alvie said.

"It's okay, they'll never know," said I , referring to our wives back at Marylou's and my apartment.

"No. I really don't want to," he said.

"You mean you don't even drink a little beer or wine?" I asked. Even as we skipped the beer and pool game, and returned home, I wasn't sure that Alvie was real. I couldn't believe that some men really didn't drink at all, and really had no secrets from their wives. But over the years Alvie proved to be one who was genuine and consistent. He had a great influence on me.

Marylou had an uncle, Alvie's brother Fritz, who was considered a "religious nut." One afternoon, Marylou and I dropped in on Fritz and his wife for a short visit when Fritz sat me down on his divan and opened his Bible, talking to me about the Lord for three hours, by the clock! I left Fritz's house confused about what he had been talking about, but mostly just glad to get away from him. As far as I was concerned, people were right: he was a religious nut, and if anyone else had approached me very soon after that with an open Bible, I would have avoided getting trapped again.

I like Fritz, and I was convinced of his sincerity, but nothing he said made any sense to me. (Years later, after I had graduated from seminary, and had many years of experience preaching and teaching the Bible, I met Fritz again, and had another talk with him. We understood each other perfectly. I came to the conclusion that in the previous three-hour diatribe he had been trying to feed meat to one who should have been fed only milk.)

I had been lying about my age since I was fifteen, and all my records were confused with the wrong birth date, March 27, 1929, and birthplace, Bergman, Arkansas. When I turned 21, legally of age, I decided to correct the records and start using my true birth date, August 13, 1931, and birthplace, Grants, New Mexico. Something else happened that year that was to straighten out other, eternal, records.

We were living in Fort Worth, Texas. Our oldest daughter, Linda, was two. Our son, Gary, was on the way, though I'm not sure we knew it yet. Alvie tried to discuss the Bible with me, but I wasn't interested. He tried to interest me in going to his church, and then my wife began to ask me to go to church with her and her folks. I wasn't aware of it at the time, but they were also praying for me.

Finally, after several weeks of invitations, in order to get them to leave me alone about it, I visited the church. There I found people who treated each other with love much like the Witnesses had treated their own. There was a difference though. These people seemed more relaxed; an air of anxiety that had been vaguely apparent in the Witnesses' Kingdom Hall was absent in the church.

The people greeted me without suspicion as if they were genuinely glad I was there. I was made to feel more truly welcome there than at any place of religious function I had previously visited.

The building seated no more than two hundred in simple, wooden pews. The raised platform was covered with a colorful, patterned carpet. Behind the pulpit was a choir area for about twenty singers. To the pulpit's left was an organ, and to the right was a piano. In front of the piano was an area, on a level higher than the main floor but lower than the platform, which seated about six musicians. Curious, before church started, I looked at the guitars and drums that had been left there and the pastor asked if I played an instrument. After my negative reply, he commented that they were always looking for people who could play.

This preacher, too, got red in the face and yelled, but the effect was not the same as it had been when I was four. This time I could understand his words, and his sermons were interesting. He preached about hell, and about people going there; and he seemed to have genuine compassion for them. He wanted to see people "saved."

"Saved" was a new term to me, but I soon understood what he meant. The preaching of hell had no effect. My years of training as a Jehovah's Witness had calloused me to any fear of eternal hell. I didn't exactly disbelieve it, nor did I believe it; I felt about the doctrine of hell like I felt about my Uncle Al—just zero, nothing.

Marylou had filled the void in my heart that only a loving wife could fill, but there was still something missing. There was still a realization that I was out of fellowship with God. In visiting the church, I got the impression that many of these folks had the same personal relationship with Deity as the man I had first heard pray, and as the old lady in the rescue mission, but it didn't dawn on me that I too could have that relationship.

The people were on a generally lower than average economic and educational level, although there were exceptions, such as my mother-in-law and father-in-law. The congregation was quite demonstrative. As the pastor preached, there were scattered responses of "amen" and "hallelujah," making an almost musical exchange between pastor and people. At the end of the sermon a plea was given for people to come forward to be "saved," or to "get right with God."

During this invitation the congregation's responses became more vocal, and often some members began to shout, and others cried out in unintelligible words of an "unknown tongue." A carpet-covered kneeling altar before the pulpit was used by people who went there to pray after the service. It was this part of the service that left my understanding far behind: a confusion of weeping, raised and waving hands, moaning, praises to God, hallelujahs, and unknown tongues.

After the third church service I attended had ended, I was filing out with the rest of the people who were exiting the building, when the pastor, who had been standing between two rows of pews at the rear of the building, reached out a hand, and gripped my arm in the same way as had the little old lady at the rescue mission.

"Joe, don't you want to be saved?" he asked earnestly. He was a tall, straight man in his early thirties. His hand tightened on my arm, and his eyes firmly held mine, demanding an answer.

"Yes," I said simply, while thinking in my heart that for me it was impossible.

"Do you want me to show you how you can be saved?" he asked.

"Yes," I heard myself saying, but still in my heart I thought there was no way for me. And I really didn't think this man could show me.

In a moment I found myself again sitting on a pew and hearing that Jesus loved me. The pastor opened his well-worn Bible, from which he had just preached a sermon, to the sixteenth chapter of Acts. He read to me how Paul and Silas had been put in jail in Philippi, how they had been locked securely in the stocks in the midst of the prison, how they had prayed and had sung hymns so all the prisoners heard them, how the Lord had shaken the prison with an earthquake so they were freed from their stocks, and how the jailor had drawn his sword to kill himself, thinking they had escaped.

"But Paul cried with a loud voice, saying, Do thyself no harm; for we are all here. Then he called for a light, and sprang in, and came trembling, and fell down before Paul and Silas, And brought them out, and said, Sirs, what must I do to be saved?" (Acts 16:28-30).

If I could have spoken face to face with Jesus Christ or the Apostle Paul, I would have asked the same question. The pastor made me realize that the message, written there in God's word, was *my* answer too: "And they said, Believe on the Lord Jesus Christ, and thou shalt be saved, and thy house" (Acts 16:31).

For the first time in my life I realized *why* Jesus Christ died on the cross: He died there to take the punishment for my sins. My sins were many, but He still loved me. Before I was ever born He loved me. He suffered there, nailed to the cross, for every sin I ever committed, to reconcile me to God. If I would believe and trust in Jesus Christ, and commit myself to His eternal keeping, depending on Him, instead of myself, He would forgive my sins. How many times before had I read that passage of scripture? But it had never soaked in. The answer to the greatest question of life now became crystal clear to me.

There I sat in a church for which I had little respect, talking to a man in whom I had no confidence, but the Holy Spirit of God had penetrated my thick head and calloused heart. I saw no blinding light. I felt no overwhelming emotional tug. But here was the answer before me in God's own word, "Believe on the Lord Jesus Christ, and thou shalt be saved." *Thou* meant me, Joe Hewitt, who was guilty of more sins than ten men my age ought to be. Jesus would come into my heart and forgive my sins, and save me if I would, believing and trusting, ask Him.

"Would you trust in Jesus Christ as your Lord and Saviour?" the pastor asked.

"Yes." That word came out immediately again.

"Let's go down to the altar, and pray," the pastor said. As we walked back down the aisle, part of me protested inside: "What are you getting yourself into?" But that small protest was soon engulfed by a great relief, that God would forgive my sins, that I could be His son, that I could have eternal life as a gift. There was no anxiety about it, no fear of failing to *endure faithfully to the end;* I was turning it all over to Christ.

As we knelt at the altar the pastor helped me to word a prayer that was already crying up to heaven from my heart in "groanings that cannot be uttered." I admitted to God that I was a sinner. I asked Him to forgive my sins, told Him I believed in Jesus Christ as my Lord and Saviour, and asked Him to come into my heart and forgive all my sins. (I did not consider the doctrine of the Trinity—to me at that point God and Jesus were somehow interchangeable terms.)

People began to gather around. Five or six began praying aloud at the same time and confusion ensued. Hands clapped my back. I felt the hot air of voices in my ear, shouting over the other noise: "Praise the Lord . . . Praise the Lord . . . Praise the Lord . . . You say, 'Praise the Lord.' "

Unidentified voices continued, first in one ear and then the other, to urge me to shout things like "Praise the Lord, Hallelujah," and "Thank you Jesus." I let out a few unpracticed, and feeble "Praise the Lord's."

"Open your mouth . . ." the group around me had not let up in their audible prayers; the hands still clapped my back. "Open your mouth . . . now start making a sound," the voice told my right ear, while others prayed loudly that I might "get the Holy Ghost."

After several minutes of my noncomprehension,

the prayer group gave up, and I was allowed up from the kneeling altar. Many people shook my hand, and commented on how happy they were that I was saved. I stepped outside and took great lungsful of the cool spring air. The time of confusion following my salvation experience was forgotten. Salvation was all settled: I was truly saved; the Almighty God had given to me eternal life. The void in my heart was now filled; Jesus was a perfect fit.

6
It Had To Be By Grace

The night of my salvation I threw away a package of Camels. The next morning I got up feeling good; the craving for a cigarette was minimal and relief from the burden of sin, and love of Jesus for my salvation were maximal.

I attended the church faithfully for three months, during which time I thought I might be called to preach, though I did not express it. I didn't smoke, drink, or cuss for a longer period than I had ever abstained from those vices since I had learned to practice them.

I was happy in the Lord, but my enthusiasm for the church that had led me to the Lord began to dwindle. Things began to get to me: the noise during church services; the group praying around an individual that he might "get the Holy Ghost . . ."; the apparent ability of some to be overcome with emotion at the flick of a mental switch, and then to return to rationality just as quickly; the preoccupation with speaking in tongues; a vague caste system, at the top of which were strong-willed women with their hair done up in tight buns, who were the most active in the shouting and tongues-speaking; a shrill-voiced evangelist with straight long hair down to her waist who seemed out of place behind the pulpit. I did not judge the church. These things just *seemed* out of place to me. I didn't know what was right to replace them, but they made me feel uncomfortable, so I decided to leave the church. Therein was great error.

I should have either stayed in that church or gone immediately to another church where I would have felt comfortable. But Satan had his way, and I got out of church completely.

Soon I resumed smoking and drinking, and gradually went back into the habits of sins of which I had so recently repented.

I stayed out of church for many years, but the Lord didn't let me have peace about it. I knew I should be living for Him, but tried not to think about it, and certainly did not admit these thoughts to anyone. One Easter, when we were living in Abilene, Texas, where I worked for the *Fort Worth Star-Telegram,* we dressed up the children, Linda, Gary, and the new baby, Debbi, and went to a large church. The pastor lambasted people who came to church only on Easter. This made me feel fully justified in staying away from church the next few Easters as well as Sundays in between.

My next experience in church was in Lima, Ohio, where I worked as a reporter, and eventually as national news editor at the *Lima News.*

As a reporter, I had talked to many preachers and church leaders. None had ever asked about my personal relationship with the Lord. The most interest anyone had taken was when my boss, Jim Dean, a Christian and a deacon, invited us to visit a small Southern Baptist church that had recently started meeting there. We went once.

While we were living in Lima, one of the greatest events in the history of the Watchtower Society took place in New York. Mama and Ray stopped and visited us on their way to the International Convention of Jehovah's Witnesses in Yankee Stadium and the Polo Grounds, where Society President Nathan H. Knorr spoke to 252,000 people in August of 1958. The urgency of witnessing in *the last days* just before Armageddon was pumped like spiritual adrenalin into the multitude.

My brother, Gordon, six years younger than I, who had been indoctrinated in the Society's doctrines from infancy, grew up, went to work for an airline, and moved to Chicago. There he met and fell in love with a lovely girl, who also happened to be a Catholic. Mama and Ray refused to go to the wedding, and never became close to Gordon's wife, Carol.

Years later they went to Chicago to visit Gordon, Carol, and their three children. Because they arrived late at night, for the convenience of all, Gordon put them up in a nearby motel. Mama and Ray confided in me later, that they thought "the priest" had told Gordon and Carol not to have Mama and Ray in their home. This was not an uncommon attitude among the Witnesses; rather it is the rule for them to see strings of manipulation running from "the hierarchy" and "the clergy" to most any source of injustice or even inconvenience.

Relations between Mama and Gordon were never the same. Often she wept and lamented her baby boy's departure from *The Truth.*

Carol was not bigoted and would have been willing for a normal in-law relationship, but Mama and Ray would not permit it. Their peer group paranoia demanded nurturing.

My wife, who during the early years of our marriage rarely went to church and claimed no religious affiliation, was much more acceptable to Mama. (Marylou was a Christian but didn't talk about it to Mama. They became good friends, and continued so even after I entered the ministry. Mama held Marylou less to blame than she did me.)

Carol, who quickly confessed her faith and trust in Jesus Christ as Lord and Saviour, and who taught her children to love and obey Him, was automatically considered to be one of the *goats*, and without hope of salvation in her present state. On the other hand, my older sister, Naomi, who was an agnostic, was several notches closer to the possibility of receiving everlasting life than Carol, according to the thinking of my mother and her religious peers.

Gordon had grown up as a Witness. His friends had been Witnesses. He was infected with their bigotry and paranoia. He was as fully indoctrinated as any person could be. Yet when he left off the steady diet of Watchtower doctrine, he drifted away from it.

The home he provides for his children is a much happier home than the one from which he came. It was not because he was not loved, but because of the *it's us against them* attitude that permeated every facet of life, and the *touch not, taste not, handle not* hyperlegalistic laws upon laws, and the *publish, witness—hurry, hurry, Armageddon is just around the corner,* religious adrenalin pumped into the heart daily.

After three years in Ohio, I bought a little weekly newspaper in Throckmorton, Texas, with a minimum down payment, part of which Ray had provided, and a large mortgage. The *Throckmorton Tribune* had been continuously published since 1885, and some of the equipment, I believe, was the original. I was located on the main east-west street of Throckmorton, population 1,299, in a dark old store building next to a smelly domino hall. There were more than a hundred drawers of handset type; ancient printers' makeup stones; two hand-fed "snapper" job presses; an old pre-World War I newspaper press—its ancient cast iron frame had been brazed, many times, these repairs looking like dentists' gold fillings—the latest patent date on the press's motor was 1914; and a Linotype machine whose date was 1909. After the deal for the paper was consummated and we had rented a house, I had only my last-ditch emergency money left, two one-hundred-dollar bills tightly folded into a pocket in my wallet.

Heretofore I had always looked forward to payday; now I dreaded it. Underfinanced as we were, making the payroll was a weekly crisis, and forced into that corner, I began to seek help from God. On one occasion after I prayed and asked God for help, my father-in-law called and asked if I needed any money. I sure did. He sent several hundred dollars and insisted that it was a gift and not a loan. On other occasions I sat at my desk with my face in my hands and asked the Lord for help to meet the obligations.

People would not have believed that I prayed. My language was foul, and I drank. I never went to church. A young man who worked for me as a Linotype operator, John Boland, was a dedicated Christian, and a member of a local Pentecostal church. John was so "narrow-minded" that he wouldn't listen to "worldly" music, so the other employees wouldn't have a radio in the shop, lest it offend him.

John would quietly ask that I set the type for movie ads, since he preferred not to be a contributor, even indirectly to such sinful activity. But he wasn't sanctimonious about his convictions, and his conversation showed a genuine love for the Lord and concern for people who did not know Him. John made me uncomfortable, but he had a lot to do with me trying to get right with God. He probably would never have guessed that I prayed.

I prayed in secret, and God answered openly. Each time, the needed money came. Often people who had owed a bill for a long period of time would suddenly pay, and the emergency would be met.

On one of these occasions of secret prayer, I became deeply convicted of how disobedient I was to the Lord. I knew Him, I was trusting Him as my Lord and Saviour, but I wasn't acting like it. I had no real assurance of salvation, because I was not living within His will, but still I knew I had a relationship with the Lord.

I prayed, "Lord, if there is a church where you

want me to go and serve, please lead me to it. I'll go, and do whatever You want me to do."

That night after we had gone to bed and I was half asleep, Marylou, as she had done often, elbowed me in the ribs and said, "Honey, we need to go to church."

"Uh-huh." I was now only a quarter asleep.

"I'm afraid neither one of us is really saved. And I'm worried about the children. We need to have them in church," she pleaded.

"Okay. We'll go," I said without hesitation. She was shocked. I didn't explain that I had already prayed and committed myself to the Lord to do so. "Where do you want to go?" I asked. (I would have gone to any.)

"Mama and Daddy have joined a Baptist church," she said. "Why don't we try that?"

"Okay. We'll go Sunday," I replied, wondering in my heart if this were God's way of answering my prayer.

That Sunday morning Marylou, all three kids, and I were in the First Baptist Church of Throckmorton. Bennie Smith, a three-quarter-size preacher, brought a full-size message on Ephesians 2:8-9, "For by grace are ye saved through faith; and that not of yourselves: it is the gift of God: Not of works, lest any man should boast." I had never heard that before. But I realized that if I really were saved *it had to be by grace.* I couldn't possibly merit salvation. It added up. Salvation was a gift, and here was a church that preached that message. It was not "earn your salvation," but trust Jesus who already earned it for you. God had answered my prayer for a church.

At the close of the sermon the congregation stood and the pastor appealed to those who would, to come and accept Christ. In my peripheral vision to the right I saw movement. It was our oldest daughter, Linda, tears flowing down her cheeks, coming toward us and the aisle. She said not a word to us, but passed in front of us to the aisle, and walked forward, and with Brother Smith helping her to pray, received Jesus Christ as Lord and Saviour.

I was embarrassed. It seemed to be a reflection on her parents, and especially on her father, who had kept her out of church all her life. But more than embarrassed, I was ashamed because it was *true*.

The next Sunday, Marylou and I both went forward for church membership and baptism.

From that time great changes came over my life. I suddenly began watching my language, and if a curse word slipped out, I was ashamed. I continued to play poker once every week or two, but I didn't enjoy it as much. One night at our poker game with friends, which included a deacon and a Sunday school teacher from the First Baptist Church, the whisky bottle was passed to me, and I declined. Everyone was surprised.

"What's the matter, Joe, you sick?"

"No, I just don't want any. Thanks." I spoke the exact truth. That night I won twenty dollars and felt terrible about it. The Lord was taking the joy out of these things, and soon I quit playing poker altogether.

I became a Sunday school teacher, and then superintendent of the Young Adults Department, a progression in church work that far outdistanced my progress in clearing up my habits.

One evening I went to the County Line to buy a case of beer (Throckmorton County was "dry"), and while I was gone the preacher came to visit.

"Where's your dad?" he asked the children.

"Oh, he's gone to the County Line."

At the liquor store, as I was going in, a deacon from our church was coming out, carrying a case of beer. We both stopped, and with shocked expressions surveyed each other.

"I didn't know you drank beer," he said.

"I didn't know you did either," I said.

When I got home the kids told me about the preacher's visit and what they had told him. I cared. Earlier I wouldn't have given a flip. I also cared about what that deacon thought of me, and I cared about my influence on him. God was changing my likes and dislikes, and within a few years, I quit drinking altogether.

We bought another little weekly newspaper in Springtown, Texas, then a commercial printing shop in Arlington, Texas, sold the paper in Throckmorton, and moved to Arlington, where we joined the Westside Missionary Baptist Church. Rayburn Blair, the pastor, was a dynamic preacher. We became good friends.

After about two years in that church, where I became more grounded in the Word of God, I gradually became more and more interested in the Lord's work. I went to church on Sunday morning, Sunday evening, and Wednesday evening, and on visitation once a week and enjoyed it. I even broke open my tight fist and began to give more than a tip to God's work, and eventually began tithing. God had a plan for my life. I began to suspect He was calling me into full-time service.

7
The Society Strikes Back

My call to preach was much like falling in love. You can't exactly explain it, but you want to be around the person you love all the time. You can hardly think of anything else except that loved one. All I wanted to do was to tell people about Jesus, to share with them what He had done for me. My printing business, which had been a struggle at the beginning, was now beginning to prosper, but I was no longer interested. I began to ask my pastor questions about seminary and Bible schools.

It took three months of the call for me to be fully convinced that it was real. The first person I told about it was Marylou. We sat down alone in the living room for a serious talk.

"I believe I've been called to preach," I said.

"I've been praying that you would be," she answered.

At the beginning of the next semester, I entered the nearest school, Bible Baptist Seminary, which was only about two miles from my shop, with the resolve that I would finish without interruption, no matter what.

I was thirty years old, and felt that I was getting a late start in the ministry. The desire to be preaching burned within me, but I felt that I had to wait until I was fully trained before starting to preach.

A long, tall, organ-playing evangelist, Dusty Rhoades, spoke in chapel at the seminary directly to me.

"If you're called to preach, go preach," he said. "Don't wait. Go preach in the jails, on the street corners, or wherever you can, but go preach!"

That's all I needed, and it's what I did. Then I began to look for a place to preach on a regular basis, and similar to the original call to preach, the Lord led me to establish a new church in Richardson, Texas, a north suburb of Dallas. Our home church in Arlington sponsored the mission, and gave us ten dollars a month token support.

For the next two and a half years, I worked for a small weekly newspaper in Richardson, first as circulation director, then advertising director, and finally as editor and publisher. I commuted to school in Arlington, and spent 7:00 a.m. to 12:00 noon in class, and I pastored the infant Trinity Baptist Church.

We had made it a practice to visit Mama and Ray in Wichita at least once a year, and usually more often. But tied up with school, the job, and the church, it was impossible for a time. Mama and Ray came to Richardson once to visit us. We were using our large two-car garage as an auditorium. We had sealed the large garage door, and had hidden it with drapery. We had covered the cement floor with scraps of carpet, and moved in homemade wooden benches that had been donated by another church. We had bought a giant old upright piano for eighty-nine dollars, and one of our members had built a sturdy pulpit. One afternoon during her visit, Mama was standing in the kitchen while we talked, near the door that led to the garage. I was proud of what we had done, and how the church was progressing.

"Here, Mama, I want to show you our auditorium," I said, opening the door to the garage.

"Oh," she said, and stepped through the door, surveying the transformed garage. Suddenly alarm covered her face. "Oh," she said again, as if frightened, and quickly stepped back into the kitchen and closed the door behind her.

"You should have told me that was your church," she said. "I should not have set foot in there."

Years later she expressed concern about it, believing it was a terrible sin for her to set foot into a church, and asked me *if I had deliberately tricked her into it.*

When we heard from Mama she would enclose Watchtower tracts in her letters. And whenever we saw her she would mention that she was praying that Gordon and I would get back in *The Truth.* I explained to her that I was saved, that Jesus Christ had come into my heart and forgiven all my sins, that I had a home in heaven, and I prayed that she too would trust in Jesus Christ as her Lord and Saviour instead of trusting in her own good works.

Usually these conversations ended with Mama in tears and Ray becoming emotional, angry, and irrational. On one occasion, I quoted John 3:16: "For God so loved the world, that he gave his only begotten Son, that whosoever believeth in him should not perish, but have everlasting life."

Ray's reply burst out, "John Three-Sixteen; John Three-Sixteen; that's all you people think about!"

On another occasion they wanted to discuss doctrine, so I suggested they pick one, and not be changing the subject. Ray decided on the doctrine of hell. I referred him to Mark 9:43-44 where Jesus said, "And if thy hand offend thee, cut if off: it is better for thee to enter into life maimed, than having two hands to go into hell, into the fire that never shall be quenched: Where their worm dieth not, and the fire is not quenched."

Ray explained that it didn't really mean eternal fire, that Gehenna, translated "hell" simply meant the dump outside Jerusalem. It made no difference what the scripture plainly said; to speak to him was like speaking to a tape recorder; he could talk, but not perceive.

I referred him to Revelation 20:10, "And the devil that deceived them was cast into the lake of fire and brimstone, where the beast and the false prophet are, and shall be tormented day and night for ever and ever." Then Ray wanted to talk about the soul. I refused. He insisted.

"Admit it," I said. "You're backed into a corner so you want to change the subject."

Ray lost his cool and, with a red face and a voice full of emotion, made heated references to my youth and how I had been deceived, and dismissed the conversation. Any religious conversation between us was counterproductive. We wanted to remain on good terms so we called a truce and agreed not to discuss religion.

Shortly after my graduation from seminary in 1965 our church moved into a new brick building on Main Street, which relieved our home from a great strain, and relieved Marylou of the responsibility of being the janitor. Our bedrooms were no longer Sunday school rooms, but just bedrooms, and the garage became just an unsanctified garage.

In 1966 Mama sent me a copy of the Watchtower book, *Life Everlasting in Freedom of the Sons of God,* which strongly implied that Armageddon would take place in early autumn of 1975. The Witnesses were not as careful in their conversations as they were in print, and many of them revealed that they were convinced that Armageddon would take place in 1975.

The book contained a *CHART OF SIGNIFICANT DATES FROM MAN'S CREATION TO 7000 A.M.* (The Society rejects the common designations of "B.C." *Before Christ,* "A.D." *Anno Domini,* or *after Christ,* and use instead, "B.C.E." *Before the Christian Era,* "C.E." *Christian Era,* and "A.M." *Anno Mundi,* or *year of the world.*)

In the chart, the history of the world was drawn up into 1,000-year "days." In the last entry, the chart lists:

1966 C.E., 5991 A.M. Threat of World War III grows more ominous as between "king of the North" and the "king of the South." (Dan. 11:5-7, 40). Expansion of organization of Jehovah's Christian witnesses continues, and international series of "God's Sons of Liberty" District Assemblies are scheduled to begin on June 22, in Toronto, Ontario, Canada. Book *Life Everlasting—in Freedom of the Sons of God* to be released Saturday, June 25, 1966.

Then:

1975 C.E., 6000 A.M., End of 6th 1,000-year day of man's existence (in early autumn).

Since the 1914 and 1925 prophetic fiascoes, the Society learned to be more careful in their wording, but the results were the same: the brainwashed multitude had forgotten 1914, and 1925, and now were fully convinced that Armageddon would take place in 1975 in early autumn. The reasoning was that the seventh "1,000-year day" would be one of rest, the Millennium.

The same book says on pages 29-30:

How appropriate it would be for Jehovah God to make of this coming period of a thousand years a sabbath period of rest and release . . . for the reign of Jesus Christ, the "Lord of the Sabbath," to run parallel with the seventh millennium of man's existence.

Oral statements were not so carefully worded: The *Arizona Republic* of August 24, 1969, quoted Erroll Burton of the Paradise Valley Unit of Jehovah's Witnesses as saying, "Within months, or at the most five years, the end of the world as we have known it will occur and a thousand year reign of Jesus will begin."

Teenage Witnesses were urged to drop out of high school so they could spend their time in witnessing before *The End*, and many did so.

A few years later I received a telephone call from a member of our church in Richardson who had not attended for at least two years. She told me that she and her husband were "studying with Jehovah's Witnesses," and wished to have their names removed from our church membership roll. I urged her and her husband to sit down and talk with me before making such a decision. She was noncommittal.

I recalled this couple. They had visited our church shortly after they were married at a young age. I had visited them many times in their apartment, and both assured me that they were trusting in Jesus Christ. The wife, however, disagreed with our church on the doctrine of baptism. Later she told me it was resolved in her mind, and they both came for church membership and baptism. They rarely attended, however.

A few months later the wife called me and asked for help. She said her husband was going out at night, claiming that he was doing undercover work for the police, and claiming that it was necessary for him to take out other women and for him to smoke marijuana. His story was ridiculous on the surface, but to satisfy her, I checked with people I knew in the police department and in the Federal Narcotics Bureau, who assured me that they had no connection whatever with this young man, and were quite amused at his story. I tried to get him to have a talk with me, but he refused.

I lost touch with them for a year or more. Then the husband called and asked that I visit him. He had moved several times since I had last been in touch with him, and now lived in an apartment in north Dallas. He was ill with the flu and troubled in his heart. In the midst of a complex of hundreds of units, in their upstairs apartment, I sat on the edge of his bed and had a long conversation with him about his drifting far from God, and the shenanigans he had perpetrated on his wife. I told him these were not the actions of a Christian, and questioned if he had ever really been born again.

He came to the conclusion that he had not ever really trusted Christ as his Lord and Saviour, that previously he had just gone through the motions. I asked him if he would then receive Christ. He said he would, and prayed in my presence, asking Christ to come into his heart and forgive his sins, and take control of his life.

Shortly thereafter he came to church and was again baptized; he came to church a few times, and that was the end of it again. I had not heard from either of them until her telephone call requesting removal from our church membership roll!

A week later she telephoned again with the same request. I told her that I was raised a Jehovah's Witness, and knew their doctrines, and pleaded with her to sit down and talk. I told her that if they became Jehovah's Witnesses they would be denying the deity of Jesus Christ, and that we would have to remove their names from our church membership roll because they had gone into heresy.

She was again noncommittal. But a few days later I received a letter from the couple, asking that I take their names off our membership roll because they were becoming Jehovah's Witnesses, and that they accepted all the doctrines of the Watchtower Society. We complied with their request, and by action of the church removed their names from our membership roll because they had entered heresy.

A few days later, I received a telephone call from a man with a British accent.

"Is this Joe Hewitt?" he asked.

"Yes."

"Is it true that you used to be a member of Jehovah's Witnesses?" he asked.

"Yes. And I would be glad to tell you why I am no longer a member of that group," I said.

"That's all I wanted to know," he said, and hung up.

I had previously heard that the Congregational Servant of the Richardson Kingdom Hall, which is located just two doors from my home, was from England. I surmised that I had just had a telephone call from him. (The *Congregational Servant* is the rough equivalent to a pastor. The Witnesses make a big to-do about not having a paid clergy, but the non-salaried *congregational servant* has little authority, and leads under the shadow of a *circuit servant* and *zone servant,* both full time and salaried, and with authority from the Society.)

About two weeks later, in January of 1972, Marylou received a letter from my mother:

> Mary will you ask Joe B. if he was ever dis-fellowshipped from the Watchtower Society of Jehovah's Witnesses. I must know. I just heard that he was, and if he was, when was it? They say he knows if he has been.
>
> Please let me know, Mary; if he has been, then other Witnesses are not supposed to talk to him and that includes me. I'm so sorry but I must do what I'm supposed to do.
>
> I have thought that by him just quitting there was no need of him being disfellowshipped. I'm so sorry if I've done wrong; may Jehovah forgive me.
>
> It's OK for me to write you or talk to you because you were never a Witness. So feel free to write, please.
>
> I love you all as ever.
> Grace.

As I read the letter, my mind raced back to the man with the British accent who had questioned me over the telephone ... back to people I had known who had been disfellowshipped and how they had come crawling back to the Kingdom Hall, repentant, and begging to be received again ... back to my dear mother; how pretty she was, how I had loved her, and how as a little boy if I thought of her dying, I couldn't bear it, and the very thoughts of it had made me cry. Now if told to do so, my mother would die *just to me,* and I would be considered by her *as one dead.*

The Society had struck back, it appeared, through my mother. I wrote to her and assured her that I had never been disfellowshipped, but if anybody wanted to bring any charges of heresy against me, I would be glad to defend myself in any Kingdom Hall or anyplace else. I would have welcomed the opportunity to defend my actions and my faith. She didn't answer my letter.

In March of 1972 Marylou and I visited Israel. While in Jerusalem I was quite moved by the experience of visiting the Garden Tomb, believed to be the place where the Lord was buried, and from which He arose from the dead. That evening in our hotel room, I wrote Mama a letter describing some of the things we had seen, wishing to share as much of the experience as possible with her. When we arrived home, the letter was there. It had been returned. I wrote again, and that letter was also returned. Now it was confirmed. My mother and stepfather would not be allowed to communicate with me.

I had left the Watchtower's religion at age 14; now at age 40, they had decided to disfellowship me in order to get back at me for labeling their converts as heretics. And in the process they broke my mother's heart.

8
"As One Dead"

Two years later, a young man, who as a teenager had been a member of our church with his family for a brief period of time, wrote me the following letter:

> Joe, I would like for you to remove my name from your records if I am still on them.
>
> You see, I have finally found the "true religion." It is one that shows true love among themselves, not just among the members of their congregation. They took a stand of neutrality and non-violence in all the wars and *any one* of the members know more about the Bible than most Baptist Deacons *and* pastors. And not only this, but they do not try and teach "doctrines of men as doctrines of God." And they worship God in "truth and spirit."
>
> Joe, do you know your God's name? The one to whom you say the Lord's prayer; "Hallowed be thy name." I don't know if you understand that it means "Sanctified be thy name . . ." That indicates that God's name should be used to identify the true God, "Jehovah." If you look in the front of your King James version you will see that almost every place Jehovah is used it is written as Lord or God. Am I mistaken or are these not titles? Many gods are mentioned in the Bible. Anyway I have been studying with some of Jehovah's Christian Witnesses for several months and I've learned more about the Bible than at any other time in my life. And the thing I like is that it makes sense now, where it didn't when I tried to make it fit what the Bap-

tists preach.

I would appreciate it if you would send me a word that you have taken me off the rolls.

His church membership had meant so little to him that he couldn't even remember which church he was a member of. My answer to his letter follows:

I am in receipt of your letter requesting that your name be removed from our church roll. Your name is not on our church roll. We had a _____ many years ago who transferred his membership to the Crestview Baptist Church in Richardson. If you are the same person, I suggest you write to that church.

I feel that it is my duty to warn you about the pit into which you are apparently falling. Since I have had much personal experience with the Watchtower Bible and Tract Society, I believe that I am qualified to do so. I was raised in that religion. In those days, however, it was not called a religion. That was a forbidden word. Neither was the "hall" or the congregation referred to as a church building or a church group. That too was forbidden by the Society.

Though we were taught to hate the Pope, the Society functioned the same as the Pope. There was a difference: the Society was a committee, not a man. The Society didn't wear long lace dresses and live in Rome, but the function was the same. Later on the Society decided it was permissible to use the words "religion" and "church" in connection with their servants.

When the Society decides a doctrine should be changed, all people who call themselves Jehovah's Witnesses immediately change their minds too. There is no individual thought, no personal freedom; like the good Catholic who believes that when the Pope speaks ex cathedra it is the voice of the personal vicar of Christ on earth, so do the Witnesses believe the pronouncements of the Society are those of Jehovah Himself!

You have been convinced that you have found "true religion." You, in fact, have been found: or in more popular vernacular, "You've been had." The measure of true religion is the Bible. The Society doesn't believe the Bible. The Bible proves so many of their doctrines wrong that many years ago it became so embarrassing that they had to come up with their own "translation," which is in fact a perversion, an alteration of the Word of God to fit their own doctrines.

All their books and pamphlets are profusely referenced to "prove" the truth of the statements. Take the trouble to look up these references. You'll find many times that the proof text is taken out of context or misapplied. Certainly there is much truth in their teachings, enough truth to serve as a vehicle for gross error.

They say that organized religion has failed to change the world, and that's true. They say that so much of Christendom is not Christian at all; and that's true. They say that Jehovah is going to put a stop to this evil system of things, that the time of the end is near; and that's true. Many of the doctrines are true, but they are used to carry error. For example, the Society and all its brainwashed servants deny the deity of Jesus Christ. They say that Jesus was a creation, and though first made, an archangel of similar rank to Lucifer. This is in clear contradiction to the Word of God in John 1:1-3, and in Revelation 1:17 and elsewhere where the Lord Jesus Christ proclaims Himself the "first and the last," and the "Alpha and the Omega, the beginning and the end."

In order to get around these truths, the Society was forced to make its own bible, changing these truths into lies.

The preaching of the cross of Christ is foolishness to them that perish. They don't understand the grace of God so they deny it. They can't understand the greatness of the Almighty, so they deny that He can and does manifest Himself to us in three Persons. They even deny the *existence* of the Holy Spirit.

You have been convinced that these hypocrites (and I use the word advisedly) practice true love to one another and to others. If the Witnesses are still like they were when I was a kid, they really do love one another. And as far as I can see, the vast majority of them are sincere in their belief, dedication, and consecration to the Society. But there is no love for others outside the fellowship. There is a pharisaical scorn for true believers in Christ, whom they make fun of for believing in the new birth. I can recall many occasions when the veteran Witnesses would laugh at and mock a faithful Christian, whose trust was in Christ, by mimicking her statement, "I've been born again."

This closed society attitude is necessary because only the initiated, the thoroughly brainwashed, or those trained from childhood, can swallow the doctrines that are so clearly opposed to God's Word. It must be a closed group because a casual visitor, who is undisciplined by the Society, might question one of the contradictions and not accept the Society's flat statement of "what that really means."

You have been convinced that these people shower true love because you've been courted.

You've been romanced. And apparently you've been seduced.

To the unbeliever who does not believe the Bible already, they appeal to his rationale: they tell him there is no place of eternal punishment, and he agrees. They tell him there is no Trinity, and he agrees. He has "found" kindred spirits who agree with him. Then gradually they brainwash him. They wash out his mind and then fill it with their own doctrines, like the man spoken of by Jesus who got rid of an evil spirit himself, his mind was swept and garnished, and then inhabited by seven even more evil spirits.

Then to the unbeliever who does believe that the Bible is true, but doesn't understand it, these Witnesses appeal to his little-but-dangerous Bible knowledge. They "reveal" to him that when he prays he doesn't know who he's praying to! He might be praying to any god when he prays to God! They show him that in the English Bible the word LORD was in the Hebrew something else entirely. "He had been lied to all these years. He has been praying to the wrong God!" They "reveal" to him that the real name of God is JEHOVAH! And the only way to be sure you get the right connection to Him in prayer is to get the address correct: "Jehovah!"

This is exciting to the Bible-familiar unbeliever and he accepts what they say. Gradually, they feed him much truth until he is indoctrinated to believing that everything the Society says is true. Then they slip him the gross doctrinal errors. Then he becomes just as brainwashed as the one to whom they appealed to rationale, and reaches the point of no return without admission of foolishness, and embarrassment.

Mr. _____, do you really believe that the Almighty Creator is tricky? Do you really believe that if you pray *to Him* in sincerity that if you don't pronounce His name right He'll direct your prayer instead to Satan? Let's not confuse God's attitudes with the Society's!

You say that the Witnesses know the Bible better than Baptist preachers. I'd love the opportunity to debate any of these "champions." They don't know what the Bible teaches. They *do* know what the Society *says* it teaches.

You seem to have been sold on the idea that because these men *say* their doctrines are not the doctrines of men they are the doctrines of God. You have apparently progressed far down the brainwash road. Look at your Bible. Compare what it says with what the Society says it says.

You suggest that I don't know my God's name. When Moses asked Him, God gave him three names: HAYAH, YHVH, and ELOHIM. These were translated into English: I AM, LORD, and GOD. The Russellites (forerunners of the Witnesses) years ago pounced on the Hebrew symbol for the Eternal God, YHVH, to which the King James translators had sometimes added vowel sounds to make it "Jehovah." The Russellites decided they had discovered the secret of tapping in to God's telephone line.

The Russellites were not the first to come to that conclusion. Jewish mystics millenniums before had taken this unpronounceable symbol for God and, by using the Hebrew letters, roughly corresponding to YHVH, spelled other words, which they believed to be magic. That was the source of most mysterious magic books that have turned up over the centuries. They believed they had located the key to tapping God's power. Now, in this "enlightened" age, so do the Witnesses.

I believe it is an insult to Almighty God to suggest that He is tricky, that if you don't know His Name you can't get through to Him. *And you don't know His Name!* If you use the King James English translation-guess for YHVH, "Jehovah," why not also use ADONI, which was translated Lord, or use ELOHIM, the plural name of deity which was translated "God" in Gen. 1:1? You don't know His Name. You guess, it is the put-together name, "Jehovah," but it could also be "Jah," or "Yahweh," or something else entirely.

The Hebrew scholars didn't feel worthy to try to pronounce the Name of God. When reading the Scripture, and they came to the holy symbol YHVH, they substituted a word they felt more worthy to pronounce, ELOHIM, or ADONI.

Men cannot be trusted with the true name of God any more than they can be allowed to look upon the true essence of God's Person. Man has a tendency to make an idol out of such things. That's why God would not allow Moses' body to be found, why He did not allow a picture of Jesus to be painted—idolatrous people would worship them. Now, like the Hebrew mystics who hoped to have a tap of God's power, the come-lately Society has decided it has an exclusive line into the Almighty. You have to be brainwashed to believe that!

"Likewise the Spirit also helpeth our infirmities: for we know not what we should pray for as we ought: but the Spirit itself maketh intercession for us with groanings which cannot be uttered. And he that searcheth the hearts knoweth what is the mind of the Spirit, because he maketh intercession for the saints according to the will of God" (Romans 8:26-27).

It's plain what the Scripture says. But what the Society *says* it says, and what the Society *says* it means, bears no resemblance to the truth.

I said earlier that I used the term "hypocrites" advisedly. Certainly people become interested in the religion of the Society in sincerity. And people enter into the brainwashing process sincerely, and I am convinced that many continue in sincerity, although they must close disciplined eyes to obvious contradictions. But in many cases, after one has been indoctrinated, brainwashed, and has so publicly committed himself to this course, he begins to see the error, but refuses to admit it because he has gone too far to back up.

For example, my dear mother has been a member of the Witnesses and a disciplined follower of the Society for 32 years. When I was nine, my father deserted us, and my mother took refuge in these friends because they convinced her theirs was the faith of her Russellite father. (I learned later from my uncle that this was not the case. Her father was quite opposed to the Witnesses' teaching against the deity of Christ.) So from the age of nine I was taught the ways of the Society. At the age of eleven I entered the "Theocratic Ministry," and began to make public talks in the meeting Hall. In school, as a disciplined Witness, I refused to salute the flag. And during World War II, I resolutely argued the Society's position against serving in the Armed Forces. At times I was beaten for these stands.

On one occasion I was attacked by six older boys who were determined that they were going

to force me to salute the flag. I was beaten,
kicked, and stomped from head to foot, but I
refused to compromise my discipline. In my
heart, I wanted to be a loyal American, because
I loved my country. At the same time, I wanted
to be loyal to my mother and to the Witnesses. I
didn't understand why these had to oppose one
another. There was in my heart the greatest conflict. I could not for myself see any violation of
the laws of God in serving my country or showing respect to my country by saluting the flag.
This made the beating harder to take. But I took
it, and from a bleeding mouth, and a tongue
covered with dirt and gravel I shouted "no" to
their demands. The thugs who tried to enforce
loyalty by such methods were much more wrong
than those people who have a sincere religious
conviction. I, as other Bible-believing Baptists,
defend the right of religious liberty, and would,
if necessary defend the Witnesses' right to
decline to salute the flag, even though I believe
their stand is wrong, and directly against the
Scriptural admonitions to be good citizens.

By the time I was 14 years old the contradictions I saw in the Society with the Scriptures
were overwhelming. It was not that I knew what
was right, but I knew that the Society was
wrong. I then considered myself a hypocrite, going along with the Witnesses to keep from hurting my mother, to keep from going back on what
I had believed, and to keep the persecutions
from having been in vain. I had since lost any
qualms about offending the leaders of the congregation because I had observed their bit-
terness toward others, and the closed society attitude. But I didn't want to hurt my mother
whom I dearly loved. This was another conflict
that had to be resolved; and the only honest way

to resolve it was to openly leave the discipline of the Witnesses. I quit going to the Hall, and quit practicing the religion. I no longer believed as they did ... and I didn't know what was right, but I knew they were wrong, and said so ... (I recounted to him my salvation experience.)

The True God is true to His promise. I was born again. I was saved. I have not always been a good son of my Heavenly Father, any more than I was always a good son of my earthly father or mother. But God changed my life. He eventually led me into a Baptist church, and called me into the ministry. I, like the servant of God in the humble church in Fort Worth, have been used by God to lead many other lost sinners into this new birth and changed life.

Now, I know what it is like to worship God in Spirit and in Truth. I pray to Him; I call Him LORD, God, Jehovah, the Almighty, my Heavenly Father; and it doesn't matter if I can properly pronounce YHVH; He hears. I belong to Him. I have been born again, "... not of blood, nor of the will of the flesh, nor of the will of man, but of God" (John 1:13).

Mr. _____, if you have not gone too far down the brainwash trail, if you still have any will of your own left, stop. Read your Bible. You will find the truth in what the Bible plainly says, not what the Society says it says.

"For the preaching of the cross is to them that perish foolishness; but unto us which are saved it is the power of God" (I Corinthians 1:18).

I never heard from the young man. About a year later I was asked to perform the wedding for one of his sisters. He came, with his wife, who had been a Witness before they married, from another state. But they did not attend the wedding itself, only the reception.

Word must have gotten around in the local community of Witnesses that I was *as one dead.* One of the members of our church, Tom Walker, worked at Texas Instruments with a woman Witness. They discussed differences in doctrines, and neither gave an inch. He would often quote something I had said, simply referring to me as "my pastor." Finally, after several of these discussions, the Witness brought Tom news at work that members of the local group of Witnesses would challenge his pastor to a debate. Tom brought the challenge to me, and I accepted immediately. The next time I saw Tom, I asked him about preparations for the debate. They had changed their minds, Tom said, after they found out who they were to debate.

"We don't debate with dead people," the Witness had told him.

9
Mama Got Her Wish

Mama had become ill in 1970 with the shingles, what she described to me as a viral infection that caused skin eruptions under her breast and around the chest to the back, and pain all the way through her body. She was too old and weak for an operation to cut certain nerves and relieve the pain, so the only thing that could be done for her was medication to help ease the pain. When we had visited her, prior to the *disfellowshipping,* she had expressed no desire to live. She bemoaned the fact that she could not get out and do witness work, and feared for her chances of the resurrection. She so much wanted to *endure faithfully to the end,* but her physical strength just didn't allow her to work.

After the breakoff of relations with me her health became worse. My oldest sister, Naomi, urged me to go see Mama in spite of the breakoff. While Mama was in a nursing home near Wichita, in May of 1974, Naomi wrote to me: "I called Mama yesterday ... Of course she was scared something had happened. Then when I convinced her that nothing had happened, then she cried. She was so happy. I told her that I had talked to you not long ago. Then she began to say, 'poor little Joe B., and sweet Joe B.,' and told me how much she loved you and Mary; and at this point I said, 'Mama, would you see Joe B. and Mary if they came to see you?' And she said, 'Of course; I couldn't turn them away.' She said, 'I think Joe B. is doing this for the money.' And I said, 'Mama, that's not true; you know how they struggled at first. And he is still holding down extra jobs to help support themselves. He believes in what he is doing. He isn't that kind of person.'

"Now *please* go to see her . . . Now Ray wouldn't approve but go anyway. This is your mother, and she loves you. She doesn't have too long to live . . . I think Ray would stop you if he could. He means well: he just thinks Mama might not be forgiven by God if she has anything to do with you . . . ."

Mama's supposing that I was in the ministry for the money was a reflection of the general attitude of the Witnesses toward any member of what they called *the clergy*. She had told me, "I don't think Gordon really believes in the Catholic church. I think he's just going along with it to keep Carol happy." To Mama, for Gordon to be a shallow hypocrite would be better than being a sincere Catholic. Now it became apparent that it would be better in the eyes of a Witness for me to be an insincere mercenary hypocrite than to really believe in what I was doing in the ministry.

Realizing that if I went to visit her against her will I might force her into a position in which she would have to compromise her convictions or turn me away . . . or that there might be a confrontation and a bad scene with Ray, I did not visit until I was invited.

Just before Christmas of 1974 I was notified that my natural father, Joseph Benjamin Hewitt, had died at the age of 85 of heart failure in Grand Junction, Colorado. The family asked me to come and preach the funeral. Mama had told me many years before that if Daddy died, she wanted to know about it. I telephoned Naomi and asked her to notify Mama, who sent word back through Naomi that Mama wanted to see me.

Marylou, our youngest daughter Debbi, and I drove to Grand Junction for the funeral. My sister Wanda came to the funeral from California, and my brother Gordon came from Chicago. After the funeral, we decided to all drive in my car to Wichita, and visit Mama. Wanda and Gordon could fly back to their homes from Wichita after our visit.

Mama was in a nursing home. Seventy-six years old, but she looked a hundred. She was thin, her hair was all gray, and pulled back, to reveal a face wrinkled by years of physical pain and spiritual anxiety. She was overjoyed to see us.

Wanda went in first, then Gordon.

"Oh, my baby, Gordon." She wept and embraced him. "Why are you wearing that beard, you look like an old man."

Marylou went in, and I followed. She hugged us all in turn, and cried with joy.

We didn't mention the disfellowshipping, but had a pleasant visit with her. Ray was his old self, cordial, and glad to see us all. Two years older than Mama, he looked as if he could have been her son. He had a full head of pure white hair; he stood straight, and moved quickly and surely.

After the initial greetings we all sat down around Mama's bed, except Ray, who left the room. Mama squeezed my hand and asked,

"Joe B., I want to die. Would it be wrong for me to want to die, and ask God to let me die?"

"No, Mama." I choked out the words.

The doctors had told her that, except for the shingles, she was in good health. Her heart was sound, her blood pressure was good, and there was no reason why she couldn't gain strength, get up from the sickbed, and live a normal life, which would help her overcome the disabling effects of the shingles. But she *wanted* to die. I was convinced that she wanted to die mainly because she couldn't do the witness work and she wanted to *endure faithfully to the end.* She had even from the sickbed telephoned people and witnessed to them so she could have a report of some kind. The Society had broken her heart; now it was killing her.

I don't claim to be a prophet, but I too made a prediction about 1975: The Watchtower Society would have a new book already printed and ready to distribute in the *autumn of 1975* in which they would smooth over the damaged expectations of the brain-washed multitude and spur them on to continue witnessing. Sure enough they issued two and a half million copies of the book *Man's Salvation out of World Distress at Hand!,* which were already printed and ready before their prophesied time of Armageddon. In a chapter, *"The Outlook After Sixty Years of World Distress,"* it suggests that members of the generation of 1914 are still alive, and *The End* doesn't necessarily have to come just yet, as long as some still survive, *this generation* has not yet passed. The book then goes on to generate alarm because of the deteriorating world conditions, using the truth of fulfilled Bible prophecies as a vehicle for their errors, but doesn't set another date for Armageddon. They'll wait a few years until the *autumn of 1975* date falls into the oblivion of 1925 and all the rest of their false prophecies.

We visited Mama again the following April, and again in September, *in the autumn of 1975.* During the September visit, for the first time I asked about why she allowed me to visit. She said, since I was not speaking out against the Society (as far as they knew) and because she was near death, "the Brethren" had given her special permission to see me.

Six months after our last visit *in autumn of 1975,* Mama got her wish. On Friday, February 20, 1976, at 5 p.m., she died of a stroke. Ray, who had been her nurse for the past six years, telephoned me, and with a breaking voice brought the news, and asked that I notify "the rest of the kids."

In a Wichita, Kansas, funeral home, the family sat together and listened to a Watchtower minister preach her funeral. Contrary to what a lot of people believed, he said, Sister Alexander would not know any conscious existence until the resurrection, at which time she would be judged, and Jehovah would determine if she was to have eternal life on earth. He preached the standard Watchtower Society doctrine: only 144,000 will go to heaven; man does not have an eternal soul; Jesus Christ died as a sacrifice for our sins, but He was a created being and His sacrifice alone is not sufficient for salvation without our works . . . .

At one point in his message, I thought he was going to back himself into a corner when he began reading from I Thessalonians Chapter 4: "Moreover, brothers, we do not want you to be ignorant concerning those who are sleeping [in death]; that you may not sorrow just as the rest also do who have no hope. For if our faith is that Jesus died and rose again, so, too, those who have fallen asleep [in death] through Jesus God will bring with him" (I Thessalonians 4:13-14, NWT). But he stopped reading there. If he had continued reading even in the Watchtower's own New World Translation of the Scripture, it would have destroyed his doctrine.

It reads: "For this is what we tell you by Jehovah's word, that we the living who survive to the presence of the Lord shall in no way precede those who have fallen asleep [in death]; because the Lord himself will descend from heaven with a commanding call, with an archangel's voice and with God's trumpet, and those who are dead in union with Christ will rise first. Afterward we the living who are surviving will, together with them, be caught away in clouds to meet the Lord in the air; and thus we shall always be with [the] Lord. Consequently keep comforting one another with these words" (I Thessalonians 4:15-18, NWT).

With verbal gymnastics the minister explained

89

that there was no burning hell, tracing back the etymology of the words "hades" and "gehenna," and taking scripture completely out of context.

He included enough truth with the message to subtly cover the error, but as usual, the truth was simply a vehicle to carry the error. I was so incensed that I could hardly keep from expressing my opinion verbally.

The Society had apparently received *New Light* on the resurrection. Previously they expected first the resurrection of the Old Testament Patriarchs. Russell said in 1907 that if the year 1915 passed without the elect's resurrection and Israel being restored, he would be proven wrong. On September 25, 1920, Rutherford predicted that the Old Testament saints from Abel to the last Old Testament prophet would be resurrected in 1925, and built a mansion for them in San Diego, California, called "Beth Sarim." Rutherford himself lived in Beth Sarim until his death in 1942.

At the close of the sermon, the audience filed out, and at the request of the family the casket was opened. My brother and sisters, and Ray gathered around the casket and wept. I had already done my weeping and grieving four years before when she had *died just to me.*

I walked to the minister, who stood alone about ten feet from the casket, and shook his hand. "I'm Joe Hewitt," I said, and motioning toward the casket, "This was my mother."

He said nothing, but nodded understandingly.

"That was a fantastic sermon," I continued. " 'Fantastic' means something 'full of fantasy.' I have never before heard such a dishonest perversion of the Word of God." I continued to grip his hand, and with measured tones finished expressing the thoughts that had been boiling in my heart throughout the sermon.

"You, sir, are not a preacher. You are a tape recorder. The Society just programs you, and when your button is pushed, you just speak what you have been programmed to speak. I suggest that you read the Bible, and believe what it says, instead of what the Society says it says, and stop taking the Scripture out of context."

On June 8, 1977, Nathan H. Knorr died, and on June 22, 83-year-old Frederick W. Franz was elected to succeed him as president of the Watchtower Society's Pennsylvania and New York Corporations.

Franz, who dropped out of the University of Cincinnati in 1914 to join Charles Taze Russell's *Bible Students,* is billed by the Society much as Russell was: "Mr. Franz, a world lecturer, in 1977 completed a lecture tour which included 11 countries extending from Ireland to Israel," the Society said.

10
Doing Away with Hell

Many people believe what they *want* to believe. Others *prefer* to believe a certain way and welcome any kind of persuasion in that direction. I know a man who has emphysema so badly that he has to keep a breathing machine in his bedroom and use it for about thirty minutes every evening when he gets home from work.

His doctor told him he had to quit smoking. So he changed doctors. The next doctor told him the same, so he changed again, and again, and again. Finally he found a doctor who told him it would be all right for him to continue smoking as long as he used the breathing machine faithfully each evening.

Another man kept changing doctors until he found one that told him he wasn't too fat. Other people run up bills until they are hopelessly in debt, and because they want to believe it, a smooth-talking "bankruptcy counselor" will easily convince them that they are fully justified in declaring bankruptcy and paying nothing, oblivious to the fact, obvious to most of us, that they are depriving others of their rightful property.

For obvious reasons there are some people who would *prefer* not to believe in hell and are receptive to any reasoning that would help convince them there is no hell. These people are ripe for the doctrines of Jehovah's Witnesses. And in due time some Witnesses will be knocking at their doors for the purpose of "picking" them.

Some criminals refuse to face the fact that prisons were built for them; and prisons are full of people who thought they were the exceptions to justice. They believed it because it's what they wanted to believe.

Other criminals, especially young ones, think, "They wouldn't lock *me* up," just before they *are* locked up.

At the same time there are rationalists who say, "God couldn't be so cruel." The rationalists too, are ripe for the Witnesses, who will be calling sooner or later.

Watchtower theology that disagrees with the cardinal doctrines of Christianity are for the most part based on taking scripture out of context. An example is in Ecclesiastes 9:5,10, which was used by Charles Russell, and continues to be used by his spiritual descendants, the Jehovah's Witnesses, to prove there is no hell.

"For the living know that they shall die: but the dead know not any thing, neither have they any more a reward; for the memory of them is forgotten" (verse 5).

"Whatsoever thy hand findeth to do, do it with thy might; for there is no work, nor device, nor knowledge, nor wisdom, in the grave, whither thou goest" (verse 10).

Let's put this into context, beginning with verse 3, and continuing with all the verses, through verse 10:

> This is an evil among all things that are done under the sun, that there is one event unto all: yea, also the heart of the sons of men is full of evil, and madness is in their heart while they live, and after that they go to the dead.
>
> For to him that is joined to all the living there is hope: for a living dog is better than a dead lion.
>
> For the living know that they shall die: but the dead know not any thing, neither have they any more a reward; for the memory of them is forgotten.

Also their love, and their hatred, and their envy, is now perished; neither have they any more a portion for ever in any thing that is done under the sun.

Go thy way, eat thy bread with joy, and drink thy wine with a merry heart; for God now accepteth thy works.

Let thy garments be always white; and let thy head lack no ointment.

Live joyfully with the wife whom thou lovest all the days of the life of thy vanity, which he hath given thee under the sun, all the days of thy vanity: for that is thy portion in this life, and in thy labour which thou takest under the sun.

Whatsoever thy hand findeth to do, do it with thy might; for there is no work, nor device, nor knowledge, nor wisdom, in the grave, whither thou goest.

Scripture must be interpreted by scripture. Any scripture that is not clear in your understanding must be interpreted by scripture which *is* clear in your understanding.

But Russell and the Witnesses have taken these two verses out of context, and have used them, in their own misunderstandings, to throw out a whole bushel of scriptures that are very clear—positively clear.

But before examining those many scriptures that clearly teach eternal punishment for sin, let's examine more closely Ecclesiastes 9:3-10. What is the recurring phrase in Ecclesiastes? "Under the sun." What is the point in these verses of scripture? Is the point there is no hell? No! The point is: Everybody has to die, and life as we know it under the sun ceases.

Notice in verse 4 the phrase "For to him that is

joined to all the living there is hope." The Watch-tower proof texts conveniently leave out "joined to all living." According to Hebrew and Greek scholars, death in the scripture means "separation." It means separation from the body; it means separation from the living, those "under the sun." The dead know not any thing: they have no consciousness on this earth, or "under the sun."

"Neither have they any more a reward" (verse 5b). There's no reward for them here, under the sun, "for the memory of them is forgotten."

Ecclesiastes is talking about life on earth here, "under the sun." Notice how the term "under the sun" recurs: "Also their love, and their hatred, and their envy, is now perished; neither have they any more a portion for ever in any thing that is done under the sun" (verse 6). When you die, you don't have any more interest in your property here, "under the sun." If you have sinned against God, and everybody has, and you die in your sins and go to hell, there's a portion for you there, but your portion on earth is gone.

"Go thy way, eat thy bread with joy, and drink thy wine with a merry heart; for God now accepteth thy works" (verse 7). It's what you do in this life that counts. Every person will be judged after this life for the things done in this life. And so ". . . there is no work, nor device, nor knowledge, nor wisdom, in the grave" (verse 10).

Certainly there is no work in the grave. What do you do in the grave? The body just rots. There's no knowledge in the grave. When you die, *you* are separated from your body, and your body goes to the grave. And *you*, your self, your personality, your soul and spirit go someplace else. There is no conscious existence in the grave, but there is conscious existence where the departed person goes. Paul said, "To be absent from the body is to be present with the

Lord." The Lord is alive, and so are those present with Him.

The Watchtower Society takes scripture out of context and tries to negate the rest of the Bible, which cannot be done. Usually at this point in discussing hell with a Witness, he wants to change the subject and talk about the soul. If you are trying to deal with a Witness, it is not advisable to allow him to change the subject. He is an expert at verbal gymnastics and will keep on changing the subject and traveling in circles. Make him stick with the subject at hand. Perhaps one of his doctrinal "partitions" will break down, and he will see one of the Society's contradictions, and become receptive to the gospel.

Four words in the Bible are translated "hell": sheol, hades, tartarus, and gehenna. In the Old Testament, the Hebrew word "sheol" means the same as the Greek word "hades" in the New Testament. Both mean "the world of the dead" or "the place of the dead," including its accessories. It means "grave," "hell," or "pit." How it is used determines its meaning.

In Ecclesiastes *sheol* is translated *grave*. That does not mean that *sheol* always means *grave*; it depends on the context. Thirty-one times the word sheol in the Old Testament is translated *hell*, and most of those times it means a place of future punishment. People who deny hell skip over these scriptures.

In Deuteronomy 32:22, Moses sang a song just before his death, speaking of the anger God had toward Israel and how that God would provoke the Gentiles at a future time: "For a fire is kindled in mine anger, and shall burn unto the lowest hell, and shall consume the earth with her increase, and set on fire the foundations of the mountains."

What was Moses talking about, a six-foot hole in the ground? No! He was talking about a place that involves fire and burning. "For a fire is kindled in mine anger, and shall burn unto the lowest hell." Not the lowest grave! That would be pointless.

Psalm 9:17: "The wicked shall be turned into hell, and all the nations that forget God." Does this mean that just the wicked are going to get buried in the grave? The scripture is talking about a place of future punishment.

Psalm 116:3: "The sorrows of death compassed me, and the pains of hell gat hold upon me: I found trouble and sorrow." There is no pain in the grave!

Psalm 86:13: "For great is thy mercy toward me: and thou hast delivered my soul from the lowest hell." What difference does it make to a dead body how deep it is buried? But the saved person, one who is in right standing with God *has* while he lives been delivered from hell, but not necessarily from the grave.

Sometimes *sheol* means grave; most of the time it means a place of future punishment. To insist that it always means *grave* would mean that there is a contradiction, but the contradiction is in the Watchtower doctrines, not in the Bible. To take two Ecclesiastes verses out of context, and try to use them to disprove the doctrine of future punishment, in the face of the above scriptures whose meaning is clear, is basic dishonesty. And for an intelligent adult to accept such verbal gymnastics as accurate, he first must have his brain washed out, and have secure partitions installed in his new Watchtower mind so that these contradictory thoughts don't touch each other. His mind has to have a degree of discipline as great as the self-sacrificing communist.

Often members of the same Christian church will have a disagreement on what the Bible means in a certain verse. Sometimes preachers of the same denomination who are good friends and whose churches are in fellowship with each other will disagree on some point of doctrine, and neither can convince the other throughout their lifetime. But I have never seen two Witnesses disagree on doctrine. I have never seen their salaried, full-time "servants" disagree with each other. Their minds are all in lockstep, and the Society is calling cadence.

The Greek word "tartarus" means "the deepest abyss of Hades," "to incarcerate in eternal torment," or "to cast down into hell." It is used only in II Peter 2:4 ". . . God spared not the angels that sinned, but cast them down into hell . . . ." It is clear from scripture that the angels that sinned are in a state of consciousness. They are not rotting in a grave. The Witnesses are preoccupied with thoughts of demon possession. I have seen them gather in little knots of three or four and talk about some *goat* to whom they have tried to witness, and one confided to the others in secretive tones, "I think he's demon possessed!" If the angels that sinned are all in graves, how can they possess anyone?

Gehenna means: "Valley of the Son of Hinnom," and "a place or state of everlasting punishment." The origin of the word was from the Valley of the Son of Hinnom, which was a place just outside Jerusalem where the pagan Canaanites made sacrifices to the gods Baal and Molech. The worship of Molech was especially abominable. The large metal idol was heated with a fire built under its outstretched arms, and the worshiper laid in those red-hot arms his own infant child as a sacrifice.

Later, the Valley of the Son of Hinnom became the Jerusalem city dump, and all kinds of refuse was taken there and burned, including dead bodies of animals and paupers. The Society tries to explain away gehenna as meaning only the Jerusalem city dump. If we took every other word back to its etymological origin and said, "That is what it means, and that only," our language would be a wreck.

It suits the Society to take gehenna back to its origin, but why not other words? For example in the New Testament, the word "spirit" is translated from the Greek word *pneuma,* meaning "breath." Sometimes *pneuma* means breath, and sometimes it means spirit. It depends on the way it is used. If we used the Society's selective logic on the word "spirit" as they have done on the word "hell," we would have to deny that God and the angels are spirits—nothing more than breath.

If we used the same logic with the Hebrew word "Messiah," which means the same as the Greek word "Christ," and both simply mean "anointed one," we would say that Christ means only *someone with oil on his head!*

To be consistent with the Society's linguistic gymnastics, nothing would mean anything. But the Society is not consistent; they pick and choose which words they wish to emasculate, to suit their own needs. Their doctrine of hell is a man-made doctrine, as are several others.

The Moslems believe hell has seven portals leading to seven divisions, that the wicked receive boiling water on their heads, drink boiling water, and suffer in eternal fire. Some Buddhists claim there is no hell; others claim there are 136 places of punishment after death. Much of what the Watchtower says Christendom believes, they took from Dante's *Inferno*, which is certainly not what Christians believe; it was just Dante's imagination.

More important than what Dante imagined, what the Society misrepresents, or what John Doe wants to believe, what really counts is *what the Bible teaches* about hell.

Future punishment is described as banishment from God. Matthew 7:23: "And then will I profess unto them, I never knew you: depart from me, ye that work iniquity." Remember, death means separa-

99

tion. The Lord is talking in this verse about future judgment after the resurrection. "Depart from me . . ." is ordering them separated from Him to another place. Therefore, the second death is eternal separation from God, and consistent with its primary meaning, separation.

Paul spoke of those that know not God and obey not the gospel in II Thessalonians 1:9: "Who shall be punished with everlasting destruction from the presence of the Lord, and from the glory of his power." It is future; it is punishment; it is separation from the Lord: it is everlasting.

Future punishment and hell are described as punishment for sin. For example in II Peter 2:4,9: ". . . cast them down to hell, and delivered them into chains of darkness, to be reserved unto judgment; . . . The Lord knoweth how to deliver the godly out of temptations, and to reserve the unjust unto the day of judgment to be punished." Though verse 4 above is about angels, verse 9 is clearly talking about people; angels are no longer being tempted, but people are. The unjust will be punished.

This future punishment will be proportionate. I have heard it said that death is a great leveler, and I agree. It doesn't make any difference how rich a man was or how poor he was, when he dies, he's equally dead. According to the Society doctrine, the worst thing that can happen to anyone is that he will be resurrected, judged, and declared a *goat,* and cast into the Lake of Fire where he will be vaporized and cease to exist. Yet the Bible teaches that this future punishment will be proportionate.

Hebrews 2:2: ". . . every transgression and disobedience received a just recompence of reward." God is just. Mass murderers like Hitler and Stalin will certainly have to suffer more for their sins than the average person who dies in his sins. Revelation 20:13: "And the sea gave up the dead which were in it; and death and hell [hades] delivered up the dead which were in them: and they were judged every man according to their works." So every man will be judged according to what he did. Punishment will be proportionate.

Hebrews 10:28-29: "He that despised Moses' law died without mercy under two or three witnesses: Of how much sorer punishment, suppose ye, shall he be thought worthy, who hath trodden under foot the Son of God, and hath counted the blood of the covenant wherewith he was sanctified, an unholy thing, and hath done despite unto the Spirit of grace?" There is, then, a sorer punishment than death, and it is proportionate.

Future punishment will be weeping and sorrow. Matthew 24:51: ". . . there shall be weeping and gnashing of teeth."

Future punishment is likened to outer darkness. Matthew 8:12: "But the children of the kingdom shall be cast out into outer darkness: there shall be weeping and gnashing of teeth." (See also Matthew 22:13.) Speaking of apostate unbelievers, Jude 13 says ". . . to whom is reserved the blackness of darkness for ever."

If one is worried about how a place can have the characteristics of outer darkness and a lake of fire at the same time, he should remember that the truth of the scripture is not dependent on our ability to rationalize it or explain it. Do these characteristics have to be experienced at the same time? And if they are, such a combination would be terrifying, especially to a blind man.

The Society also picks and chooses when to rationalize. I have heard Witnesses question sarcastically, "Who's going to keep the fires of hell going while the devil is chained in the bottomless pit?" Their ignorance sticks out like a sore thumb. They have believed that *organized religion is a snare and a racket,* they have lumped all churches who claim to be Christian into one corrupt body they call *Christendom,* which is led by *demon-possessed,* greedy men, *the clergy,* who teach the *doctrines of men* rather than the doctrines of God. They have believed that all *Christendom* accepts Dante's *Inferno* as dogma, that the devil tends the fires of hell assisted by demons with horns, tails, and pitchforks. This is the same kind of logic that would say all who are not communists are fascists.

Hell is a place people go to after death, and it is to be feared. Luke 12:4-5: "And I say unto you my friends, Be not afraid of them that kill the body, and after that have no more that they can do. But I will forewarn you whom ye shall fear: Fear him, which after he hath killed hath power to cast into hell [gehenna]; yea, I say unto you, Fear him." These were the words of Jesus, and they are the basis for much of the common Christian understanding of the doctrine of hell. Jesus said plainly that after men have killed the body there is no more they can do—taking the body to the Jerusalem city dump and allowing worms to eat it, or burning it with fire, means nothing to a person who has died. Yet Jesus said it is to be feared what He can do *after* that person is dead, because Jesus has the power to cast that *person,* not his old lifeless body rotting in the grave or in some city dump, but that *person* into hell. Hell is a place to be cast into, and, according to Jesus Christ, it is to be feared, whereas what man can do to you after you are dead is not to be feared.

The future punishment is everlasting punishment. Matthew 25:46: "And these shall go away into everlasting punishment: but the righteous into life eternal." The Society chooses to make one of these states truly everlasting: "life eternal," and the other they choose to mean cessation of existence: "everlasting punishment." The Watchtower

Society's own Bible, in which they have arbitrarily changed the meaning of many words to fit their own doctrine, renders this verse: "And these will depart into everlasting cutting-off, but the righteous ones into everlasting life" (Matthew 25:46, NWT).

The Watchtower's *Diaglott,* Greek and English New Testament, has the Greek word *kolasin* translated "cutting off," while others translate that same Greek word "punishment" or "torment." I have five other English translations of the Bible in my library. All except one says "punishment," and the exception says "torment."

Daniel 12:2: "And many of them that sleep in the dust of the earth shall awake, some to everlasting life, and some to shame and everlasting contempt." Shame and contempt would have no effect on one who was just resurrected long enough for a trial and then, fried; but shame and contempt certainly are to be feared, being everlasting.

The Bible teaches that this future punishment is hell fire. Matthew 5:22: ". . . but whosoever shall say, Thou fool, shall be in danger of hell fire [gehenna]," Jesus said. Those are His words, not mine. I believe Jesus knew for sure! Matthew 13:42: "And shall cast them into a furnace of fire: there shall be wailing and gnashing of teeth." You don't wail and gnash your teeth in the grave, or after you've been fried. Matthew 25:41: "Then shall he say also unto them on the left hand, Depart from me, ye cursed, into everlasting fire, prepared for the devil and his angels." Why did Jesus call it *"everlasting fire"* if it were not *everlasting?*

If it were not so tragic, the Society's explanation of the account in Luke 16 of the Rich Man and Lazarus would be downright funny. The Bible says: "There was a certain rich man, which was clothed in purple and fine linen, and fared sumptuously every day: And there was a certain beggar named Lazarus, which was laid at his gate, full of sores, And desiring to be fed with the crumbs which fell from the rich man's table: moreover the dogs came and licked his sores.

"And it came to pass, that the beggar died, and was carried by the angels into Abraham's bosom: the rich man also died, and was buried; And in hell [hades] he lift up his eyes, being in torments, and seeth Abraham afar off, and Lazarus in his bosom. And he cried and said, Father Abraham, have mercy on me, and send Lazarus, that he may dip the tip of his finger in water, and cool my tongue; for I am tormented in this flame.

"But Abraham said, Son, remember that thou in thy lifetime receivedst thy good things, and likewise Lazarus evil things: but now he is comforted, and thou art tormented. And beside all this, between us and you there is a great gulf fixed: so that they which would pass from hence to you cannot; neither can they pass to us, that would come from thence.

"Then he said, I pray thee therefore, father, that thou wouldest send him to my father's house: For 1 have five brethren; that he may testify unto them, lest they also come into this place of torment.

"Abraham saith unto him, They have Moses and the prophets; let them hear them. And he said, Nay, father Abraham: but if one went unto them from the dead, they will repent. And he said unto him, If they hear not Moses and the prophets, neither will they be persuaded, though one rose from the dead" (Luke 16:19-31).

This passage of scripture is not difficult to understand; it simply means what it says. But it becomes difficult to understand if it has to fit a preconceived doctrine such as the Watchtower's doctrine on hell. According to the Watchtower's book, *The Truth That Leads to Eternal Life,* this passage of scripture is a parable illustrating the torments false religious leaders suffered when Christ's followers after Pentecost exposed their evil words. Could anyone accept that without first being brainwashed?

God did not cause the Bible to be written to confuse us but to enlighten us. Jesus didn't tell the account of the Rich Man and Lazarus to confuse us either, but to convey to us the truth about what happens after death, paradise for some, and torment for others, depending on whether they repent.

The Watchtower arbitrarily claims the passage is a parable. But Jesus said there was a *certain* rich man. He said there was a *certain* beggar, and gave that *certain* beggar's name, *Lazarus.*

Lazarus was destitute. Verse 22 says he died, but doesn't mention that he was buried. These are strong indications that, as a pauper, his dead body was hauled off to the Jerusalem city dump to be eaten by worms and burned. But the Rich Man was buried. To be consistent with Watchtower doctrine and verbal gymnastics, we would have to conclude that Lazarus went to *gehenna,* and the Rich Man went to *hades!* But the real truth is what happened to *their bodies* is just incidental to the point the Lord is making, *which is what happened to their person apart from their bodies.*

After Lazarus' body was hauled to the Valley of the Son of Hinnom, Lazarus himself went to paradise "into Abraham's bosom." This was an allusion to a custom which was to seat the guest of honor on a reclining couch at the banquet table next to the lord, prince, or king. This would put the honored guest's head nearest the bosom of the host.

After the Rich Man's body was buried in a grave, probably following an expensive funeral, the Rich Man himself was in torment. In life "under the sun" the Rich Man had not believed the Bible, "Moses and the prophets." Tormented by the flames he realized his error. It was too late for him—none could cross the gulf—but he was concerned about his five brothers, who were still alive "under the sun" and who could still believe and repent. (So could the false religious leaders after Pentecost; and many of them did believe and trust in Jesus Christ, the Apostle Paul, for example, which makes the Watchtower's explaining-away of these scriptures even more ridiculous.)

One of the main points of Jesus' message in this passage of scripture is that we have the Bible; if we don't believe what it says, we wouldn't believe though one were raised from the dead (and Jesus Himself was raised from the dead). We must believe and trust in the Lord now in this life "under the sun;" when we die it's too late to cross over from eternal torment to eternal life.

Revelation 20:15: "And whosoever was not found written in the book of life was cast into the lake of fire." Revelation 20:10: "And the devil that deceived them was cast into the lake of fire and brimstone, where the beast and false prophet are, and shall be tormented day and night for ever and ever." John the Baptist said in Matthew 3:12: ". . . but he will burn up the chaff with unquenchable fire." Revelation 14:11: "And the smoke of their torment ascendeth up for ever and ever: and they have no rest day nor night . . ." If we believe the Bible, we must believe what it says: there is future punishment for un-forgiven sin; it is everlasting punishment; it involves separation from God, and torment; and it involves a place.

". . . Judas by transgression fell, that he might go to his own place" (Acts 1:25).

The Watchtower's hell-denying doctrine is a nar-cotic to numb the minds of people headed there, so they won't repent and believe the gospel.

11
A Thimbleful of Understanding About the Trinity

In an attempt to illustrate the impossibility of understanding God, somebody said, "You can't put the Pacific Ocean in a thimble," and that is true, but you can put *some* of the Pacific Ocean in a thimble. No finite human being can completely understand God, but we can understand *some* of God and for that reason God has given us His Word. So we ought to learn from His Word and understand what we can. We can at least get our "thimble" full.

The word "trinity" is not in the Bible. There was no theological formula of the Trinity published until A.D. 335. People didn't need it; they just read the Bible and believed it. That is what we ought to do today. Trouble in understanding the Trinity arises when men try to change God to fit their own understanding.

In history, there have been those who, because they could not understand the Trinity, denied it. Arius of Alexandria in the Fourth Century A.D. believed that Christ and the Holy Spirit were created beings, but he believed Christ should still be worshiped. The Arian doctrine is not dead today; it is still promoted by various cults. The Mormons have a sort of quasi-arian doctrine: they believe that Jesus Christ was created. The old Unitarians, who believed in God, believed that Jesus was a created being, but they said no created being should ever be worshiped. (I think they were right; no created being should be worshiped, but Jesus Christ was not created.) They said they worshiped God only, and since they denied the deity of Christ they denied Him worship.

Back in the early days of Christianity a group called "Socinians" believed that Jesus Christ was man only, and that the Holy Spirit was simply an influence. Their doctrine has been passed down to the present time. These people cannot understand how Jesus Christ could take upon Himself temporary humility.

Jesus said, "All power is given unto me in heaven and earth." If Jesus Christ was not God, He could not have received all power. Why did He receive all power? Because He had voluntarily *given up* all power when He came to earth in humility to be born in a barn. They cannot understand the humility of Christ.

We read the Bible and understand that Jesus Christ, in His humility, did not know some things. God knows everything; but Jesus Christ laid aside free exercise of His attributes. He said, speaking of His second coming, "Of that day or that hour knows no one, not even the angels in heaven, not even the Son, but the Father." There were some things He didn't know.

Jesus suffered physical fatigue. When He went into Samaria and came to Jacob's Well, "Jesus therefore, being wearied with his journey, sat thus on the well" (John 4:6). He was tired. And the modern-day Arians and Socinians strangle on this. They cannot understand how God the Son could lay aside the free exercise of His power and come to earth in temporary humility.

We cannot alter God to fit our understanding. But they try; they keep on trying. In Philippians 2:7, the Word of God says that Jesus emptied Himself, taking the form of a servant, being made in the likeness of men. He did it Himself; He voluntarily emptied Himself and was made in the likeness of man. When He said in John 14:28, "My Father is greater than I,"

He meant it. He had come in temporary humility.

There is another extreme. Some people read John 1:1 and they see: "In the beginning was the Word, and the Word was with God, and the Word was God . . ." and they say, "Jesus was God," and they deny His humanity. Extremists on the other end of the spectrum try to change God to fit their own understanding and deny the Father and Holy Spirit. The lunatic fringe goes all the way around.

A man called me on the phone from a nearby city and asked if I was aware of certain things wrong with the world which he began to enumerate. Then he started telling me about things that are wrong in "the churches."

He had been going on for ten minutes when I said, "Tell me something I don't know," and finally succeeded in getting him to his point.

He said, "I want to know: do you baptize in the name of Jesus?"

"Yes we do baptize in the name of Jesus."

He said one of the things wrong with churches today is that they baptize in the name of the Father and the Holy Spirit.

I said, "Do you have a Bible there?" He did, so I asked him to turn to Matthew 28:19. I said, "This is the way we do it: ' . . . baptizing them in the name of the Father, and of the Son, and of the Holy Ghost.' "

"That is not what it means," he said. "You're supposed to baptize in the name of Jesus only."

I said, "Will you please turn to Matthew 28:19, and read it again."

The Bible means what it says, and I believe it. Some people think, "Because I can't put the Pacific Ocean in a thimble, I refuse to believe there *is* a Pacific Ocean." Isn't that ridiculous? Because I can't comprehend, in my little thimble brain, that God is one God manifest in three persons does not mean I should get off in left field and deny what the Bible plainly says about the deity of Jesus Christ. Nor does it mean I should get off in right field and deny the Holy Spirit and the Father. People who are so faithless are trying to make God fit the limits of their understanding.

If we made everything fit the limits of our understanding, I personally would have to do without electricity, because I don't understand it, and because of my limited understanding, find it difficult to believe anybody understands it.

We'd have to do without gravity. I can't understand magnetism. My three-year-old granddaughter was playing with a magnet. I demonstrated that it would stick to iron and wouldn't stick to anything else. We went around the house demonstrating that it wouldn't stick to wood, brass, aluminum, plastic, fabric, or glass. We put the magnet on several objects to see if they had iron in them. I asked her what a magnet would stick to, and she said "i-ron." She knows about magnets and iron; I know about magnets and iron, but neither of us really understands it. But I accept it. I see the evidence; it sure enough sticks. I've heard it explained, and read about it, but I still don't understand why the magnet sticks to iron, but that doesn't keep it from sticking.

If we had to fit everything to our understanding, most of us would do without color television. Some of us would do without black and white TV and radios too.

Probably there are some people today sitting around muttering, "I don't think they really did go to the moon." If the space program was limited to my understanding, they never would have gone, but because of the evidence, I believe they did.

If we had to make everything fit the limits of our understandings, nobody would farm, because who can understand how life comes from a seed? During

World War II in London there were buildings bombed that had covered the earth for 400 years. The bombing had destroyed the buildings so with bulldozers they scraped off the rubble allowing the sun to reach that soil. There came grass and flowers from seeds that had been dormant for centuries.

I'm glad farmers don't have to limit their belief to their understanding. Yet, this is what people will do with God. They say, "Let's let God fit only the limits of our understanding," so they believe in a *little* god.

The Bible tells us what we ought to know about God. First of all in order to at least get a thimbleful of understanding about the Trinity is to understand that God is one God. Some of the modern-day Arians, the *Jehovah's Witnesses* for example, accuse Christians of believing in three gods, but it is a misrepresentation. Christians do not believe in three gods; Christians believe in one God. Deuteronomy 6:4 says, "The Lord our God is one Lord." Our God is one God. Jesus quoted this in Mark 12:29. The apostles certainly believed in the unity of God. The Apostle Paul, in I Corinthians 8:4 said, "There is none other God but one."

The word "trinity" is not there, but if you look in the Old Testament, you see the Trinity. In the very first verse in the Bible we see, "In the beginning God created the heaven and earth." That word God, in the Hebrew, is "Elohim," which is plural. Knowing the unity of God, that God is one God, the translators rightly used "God," instead of "Gods." The God spoke and Creation resulted. "And the Spirit of God moved upon the face of the waters . . ." (Genesis 1:2). Here we have the Holy Spirit involved in creation. Then in Genesis 3:8, after Adam and Eve had sinned against God, we have God the Son, or the Word: "And they heard the voice of the Lord God walking in the garden . . ." Who was that, the voice of the LORD, Jehovah? God the Son. We don't get beyond three chapters of the book of Genesis until we see the Father, the Son, and Holy Spirit; one God, manifest in three persons.

Many times in the Old Testament God refers to Himself in the plural. Genesis 1:26: "Let us make man in our image."

Isaiah 6:8: "Also I heard the voice of the Lord, saying, whom shall I send, and who will go for us?"

When the people became disobedient and built the tower of Babel, God said, "Let us go down, and there confound their language" (Genesis 11:7).

Throughout Genesis theophanies appear. A theophany is a manifestation of God in the flesh, a preincarnate form of Jesus Christ. "No man hath seen God at any time; the only begotten Son, which is in the bosom of the Father, he hath declared him" (John 1:18). So when an angel of the Lord stood before a man and said in first person, "I, the LORD," who was speaking? No man has seen the true essence of God, so anytime we see God in the flesh, we are seeing God the Son. God's Word does not contradict itself.

The angel of the Lord appeared to Hagar, the maid of Sarah and Abraham, and spoke to her in the first person in Genesis 16:10: "And the angel of the LORD said unto her, I will multiply thy seed exceedingly." Here was God in the form of a man speaking to an individual human being.

Three men appeared to Abraham who called one of them LORD. That word in all capital letters means Jehovah, LORD, the Self-existent One, the Eternal God, and He appeared as a man. That was God in the flesh, Jesus Christ in a preincarnate form. He spoke to Abraham. In Genesis 18:14 He said, "Is any thing too hard for the LORD? At the time appointed I will return unto thee, according to the time of life, and Sarah shall have a son." This was not a man making this promise, it was God; it was the LORD, Jehovah;

this was Jesus Christ in a preincarnate form.

Dennis Jackson, a Jehovah's Witness high school student, was asked to write a paper on some person that he greatly admired. He chose Jesus Christ. Where was he to get information on Jesus Christ? He didn't get it from Watchtower literature, but went to the Bible. What he read there had a tremendous impact on him; it confused him, because it was so opposed to his Watchtower training. But he shook it off and continued as an obedient member of the brainwashed multitude.

Years later somebody put on his car windshield a tract by John R. Rice, "What Must I Do To Be Saved." He and other Witnesses in the car read it and laughed at the idea of salvation by grace. He threw away the tract, but he didn't forget its message. Something had happened to him; it was like the time when he had written the theme on Jesus Christ, but he shook it off again.

Later he found another of those tracts, "What Must I Do To Be Saved." Again he read it. The Holy Spirit who had started to work in his life when he got into the Bible as a high school student, now finished the job, and the young man received Christ as his Lord and Saviour.

Then he became excited about it. He had been saved! He had Christ in his heart, and he wanted to tell his Witness friends. He told them about his newfound faith and his belief that Jesus Christ, and the Holy Spirit, and the Father are one, and of his salvation by grace.

These things appalled his friends. He *knew* he was going to heaven. And they couldn't stand that either. He invited his Witness friends to sit down and talk about it, but nobody wanted to. Finally he got his assistant congregational servant to invite him to his home and talk about it. They began to go into the Scriptures. In Genesis 18:14 the new Christian read about God in the flesh, that Abraham spoke to Jehovah and Jehovah spoke back to Abraham.

The assistant congregational servant turned pale; his jaw dropped, and he said, "We can't help you, I can see that the Devil has got you hook, line, and sinker. This is my house and I order you to leave." (Dennis Jackson's story is available in a booklet, *From Darkness to Light*, published by Missionary Crusader, Lubbock, Texas.)

Even in the Watchtower's own version of the Bible, they were not able to cover up all of the truth, that God could be on earth in the form of a man and be in heaven at the same time . . . that God could be one God, yet He could be the Father, Son, and the Holy Spirit, all at the same time.

The Trinity is also taught in the New Testament. At the baptism of Jesus we have all three persons of God present. Matthew 3:16,17: "And Jesus, when he was baptized, went up straightway out of the water; and, lo, the heavens were opened unto him, and he saw the Spirit of God descending like a dove, and lighting upon him: And lo a voice from heaven, saying, This is my beloved Son, in whom I am well pleased." Here we have the Father speaking from heaven, the Holy Spirit descending like a dove, and God the Son, who had come in temporary humility, being baptized.

Jesus believed in the Trinity. Jesus in John 14 spoke of the Comforter who was to come. In John 14:16-18, He said, "And I will pray the Father, and he shall give you another Comforter, that he may abide with you for ever; Even the Spirit of truth; whom the world cannot receive, because it seeth him not, neither knoweth him: but ye know him; for he dwelleth with you, and shall be in you. I will not leave you comfortless: I will come to you."

We might look at this and understand that Jesus would not leave the disciples comfortless: He would send another Comforter, the Holy Spirit, to be with them forever, then later He, Jesus Christ, would return.

Jesus mentioned again the Comforter, the Holy Spirit, who was to come, in John 14:26, "But the Comforter, which is the Holy Ghost, whom the Father will send in my name, he shall teach you all things, and bring all things to your remembrance, whatsoever I have said unto you." Jesus believed in God being manifested in more than one person. He mentioned all three persons of God in the great commission, "Go ye therefore, and teach all nations, baptizing them in the name of the Father, and of the Son, and of the Holy Ghost" (Matthew 28:19). Jesus believed in the Trinity.

Paul believed in the Trinity; he said in II Corinthians 13:14, "The grace of the Lord Jesus Christ, and the love of God, and the communion of the Holy Ghost, be with you all."

Peter believed in the Trinity. He said in I Peter 1:2: "Elect according to the foreknowledge of God the Father, through sanctification of the Spirit, unto obedience and sprinkling of the blood of Jesus Christ: Grace unto you, and peace, be multiplied."

The Book of Revelation is from God the Father, Son, and Holy Spirit. "The Revelation of Jesus Christ, which God gave unto him . . ." (Revelation 1:1); ". . . and from the seven Spirits which are before his throne" (Revelation 1:4); "And from Jesus Christ, who is the faithful witness, and the first begotten of the dead . . ." (Revelation 1:5). The message of Revelation is from the Lord God, much of which is in the first person. Fifty-five times when the Lord uses the word "I," it is irrefutably the Lord Jesus Christ speaking.

The message of Revelation is from all three persons of God, but it is spoken to John in the first person, by Jesus Christ, the same as the LORD who appeared to

Abraham as a man and spoke to him in the first person, and the same as the Angel of the LORD who spoke to Hagar, and others in the Old Testament in the first person.

The word "trinity" isn't so important; we don't pray "Holy Trinity," we pray to God. When you pray you might say, "Our Father which art in heaven . . ." You might pray, "In the name of Jesus Christ, Father, do this for me . . . give me this blessing . . . ." We pray through Jesus Christ, and Jesus and his Father are one. We might pray, "Dear Jesus, be with us and bless us." We might pray, "O Holy Spirit, empower us to be real witnesses to You." Who are we praying to? We are praying to the one God, indivisible, yet manifest to us in three persons.

To deny the three persons of God is to put a limit on God, and demonstrate a lack of faith. God could have been four persons; that would not have been difficult for the Almighty God. God could have been one God manifest in a hundred persons if He took a notion. We can't limit God; He is one God, but He is not limited. The eternal God eternally is, has been, and will be, three persons—the Father, the Son, and the Holy Spirit. Don't try to shrink the Almighty God into the thimble of your own understanding. When we realize how small we are, our own unrighteousness, sinfulness, and unworthiness, and we accept Jesus Christ as our Lord and Saviour, we begin to have a little more understanding about God. We begin to see how great He is. Think about how small this little planet is, and indeed even this solar system. Think about how small we are on this little planet. Then look at the universe and realize God is the Creator of it all, and Sustainer of it. He is so great, we cannot understand all of God, but we can understand *some* of Him by believing what the Bible says, not what someone says it says.

12
The 144,000: Are There Classes of Salvation?

The Lord Jesus Christ spoke of a Gentile, who had demonstrated great faith: "And I say unto you, That many shall come from the east and west, and shall sit down with Abraham, and Isaac, and Jacob, in the kingdom of heaven" (Matthew 8:11). In the future, from the day that Gentile lived, there would be many people from many parts of the world in the kingdom, and they would sit down in heaven with the Old Testament saints. Therefore, both old Testament saints and saints who lived later, went to heaven.

Yet the Jehovah's Witnesses and some other cults believe that salvation in heaven is not available to everybody, that there are certain people not eligible. For example, until recent *new light* was received by the Mormons, a black person was prohibited from the priesthood, temple ordinances, and subsequent "exaltation" in the highest Mormon heaven. And the Witnesses believe that only 144,000 people will go to heaven. They believe anybody else that earns salvation will be eligible to live eternally on earth, but he cannot go to heaven. These cults believe in classes of salvation.

When we talk about salvation, we are talking about being saved *from* the penalties of our sin *to* eternal life. There are many other kinds of salvation: If somebody reaches down and grabs a drowning man by the hair of his head, and pulls him out of the water, he has saved the man from drowning. Nobody is half saved from drowning. He may feel as if he's half drowned, but he's not. You can be saved from sickness; you can be saved from death by fire in your home. But when the Bible speaks of being saved, or salvation, it is speaking of being saved from eternal death to eternal life.

According to the Scriptures there are only two kinds of people in this respect, saved people and lost people. John 3:18: "He that believeth on him is not condemned: but he that believeth not is condemned already, because he hath not believed in the name of the only begotten Son of God." Either you're condemned or you're not condemned. (See also John 3:36 and John 10:28.)

According to the Bible, salvation is available to all who will repent and believe in Christ. John 3:16: "For God so loved the world, that he gave his only begotten Son, that whosoever believeth in him should not perish, but have everlasting life." *Whosoever* means *you* whether you're one of the 144,000, a Jew, Gentile, Black or White. Acts 2:21: "And it shall come to pass, that whosoever shall call on the name of the Lord shall be saved." Romans 10:13 says the same: "For whosoever shall call upon the name of the Lord shall be saved." *Whosoever* believes and calls on the Lord shall be saved.

God wants everybody to be saved. I Timothy 2:4 says, speaking of God, "Who will have all men to be saved, and to come unto the knowledge of the truth." And if a person is not saved, it is not God's fault, because God has provided a way to salvation.

The free gift of salvation was available to all men. Romans 5:18: "Therefore as by the offense of one judgment came upon all men to condemnation; even so by the righteousness of one the free gift came upon all men unto justification of life." God is no respecter of persons. The Bible does not teach classes of salvation; there is no heaven for dark people and another heaven for light people. The Bible certainly doesn't teach that there is heaven for 144,000 special people, including the Watchtower hierarchy, and that no one else is even eligible.

The Watchtower Society uses Revelation 7:4 to prove that only 144,000 will go to heaven. John said, "And I heard the number of them which were sealed: and there were sealed an hundred and forty and four thousand of all the tribes of the children of Israel." Now does that say to you that only a hundred and forty-four thousand people are going to heaven? No, it says that there were sealed 144,000 people of *the children of Israel.* It doesn't say anything about them being the only people going to heaven. And then it goes on to say, "Of the tribe of Juda were sealed twelve thousand ..." and then lists eleven more tribes from each of which would come twelve thousand: Reuben, Gad, Aser, Nephthalim, Manasses, Simeon, Levi, Issachar, Zabulon, Joseph and Benjamin.

The hierarchy of the Watchtower Bible and Tract Society believe they are of the 144,000 which they also call "the elect." I recall three people (there were probably more) in the Kingdom Hall I attended who believed they were of *the elect.* One was my uncle, another was a very active man in the congregation, and the third was a woman who came to the Hall only once a year for the Lord's Supper.

I wonder which tribe of Israel Uncle Al was from? His progenitors came from Ireland and Scotland. He had not a drop of Hebrew blood. He couldn't claim any of these tribes. I wonder which tribe the other Gentile "members of the 144,000 thousand" belong to?

The elect, the 144,000, also called the *little flock, ideal Israel, spiritual Israel* and the *anointed remnant,* is dwindling, most by death. But some, by becoming unfaithful, had to be replaced, according to the Watchtower book, *Life Everlasting—in Freedom of the Sons of God.* The second-class Witnesses began to be actively recruited in 1934, and were called the *other sheep* or *Jonadabs.*

That was the year the Watchtower officially declared: "It was Scripturally fitting for these 'other sheep' (pictured by the faithful Jonadab of ancient time) to dedicate themselves to Jehovah God and get baptized .... Since then, almost a million persons have dedicated themselves to Jehovah God and have been baptized in water and now profess to belong not to the anointed remnant of the 'little flock,' inasmuch as the bringing in of the 'other sheep' had begun only recently." In 1948 "there were 376,393 reported attending the Lord's evening meal, and, of these only 25,395 partook of the emblematic loaf and wine, to indicate they were of the anointed remnant. However, in the year 1965, at the celebration ... 1,933,089 attended, but only 11,550 partook. Thus 13,845 of the faithful remnant of the 'little flock' passed from the earthly scene in a matter of seventeen years (1948-1965).

"It is possible that some baptized Christians were added to the anointed remnant, not to increase the number, but to replace any of them who had proved unfaithful to the heavenly calling and who therefore leave a vacancy to be filled .... But despite the bringing in of such ones as replacements, the number of the anointed remnant kept decreasing because more of these died faithful and were taken into the heavenly kingdom than the number of replacements brought in" (pages 148-149).

When I was a Jehovah's Witness, I believed that only 144,000 were going to heaven, not because it was in the Bible, but because that was what I was told. How does any Jehovah's Witness know that only 144,000 are going to heaven? Because that's what the Society told him. Not one of the brainwashed is allowed to think for himself.

The Watchtower Society tolerates no difference of opinion on doctrine among its disciples. An example of this is found in a book by Charles Trombley, entitled *Kicked out of the Kingdom* (Whitaker House, Monroeville, PA, 1974). In it Trombley told how he was evicted from the Watchtower Society because he and his wife prayed that their little girl's clubfeet would be healed, and the child was miraculously healed overnight. Jehovah's Witnesses are not allowed to believe in any kind of divine healing, and they are taught that any miraculous healing today is of the devil. You've really got to tear the Bible apart and paste it back together again to suit yourself to believe that!

Another text the Society uses to "prove" their "144,000" doctrine is in Revelation 14:3 which speaks once again of these 144,000 specially chosen Jews, "And they sung as it were a new song before the throne, and before the four beasts, and the elders." These things will take place in heaven. We know that the 144,000 will be redeemed from the earth, during the great tribulation ". . . and no man could learn that song but the hundred and forty and four thousand, which were redeemed from the earth."

Now the Society says that means only 144,000 are going to go to heaven. Read more of the description of this 144,000 from the twelve tribes of Israel: "These are they which were not defiled with women, for they are virgins." They are all to be men, and all virgins—they've never been married, never been guilty of fornication. None of the *Elect* I ever knew of would fit that description! For example my uncle had been married twice and had many children.

Visiting in the home of a man I hoped to win to the Lord, I was told that he had been "studying with Jehovah's Witnesses." I asked what he thought about what they were teaching.

"Some of it is quite different," he said, "but they

back it up with the Bible. Whatever they say in their books they have scripture references right there to back it up."

That was the impression the Society desired to leave. I can remember when I was a Witness "witnessing" to people and challenging them to look up the references. Most people never bother, especially when challenged to do so. An abundance of references is impressive. The man I visited hadn't bothered to look them up either.

Usually a flat statement is made, such as, "Did you know that only 144,000 chosen from among mankind over the past nineteen centuries would gain heavenly life? And did you know then that the Bible holds out hope of eternal life under righteous conditions here on earth for all others who would become faithful servants of God?—Psalm 37:10, 11, 29, (36:10, 11, 29 Dy)" (from the Watchtower book, *The Truth that Leads to Eternal Life,* page 79).

The casual reader would assume that the scripture references listed were to back up the statements made. The cited references, Psalm 37:10,11, 29 read, "For yet a little while, and the wicked shall not be: yea, thou shalt diligently consider his place, and it shall not be. But the meek shall inherit the earth; and shall delight themselves in the abundance of peace . . . The righteous shall inherit the land, and dwell therein for ever." Does this prove that only 144,000 will go to heaven, and that the rest of the saved will have no hope for heaven, but will live instead on the earth? Often the statement regarding the 144,000 is made and the scripture references, Revelation 7:4, 14:1-3, are thrown in. But as we have seen, those scriptures don't say it either.

Apparently the Bible's listing the 12,000 out of each of twelve tribes of Israel, and the Bible saying that they would all be male Jews, and virgins, has proved such a source of embarrassment to the Society that they decided to meet the problem head-on, and boldly quote the listing on page 33 in the Watchtower book, *Man's Salvation out of World Distress at Hand!* Following the brassy listing of the tribes, this explanation is given: "The number of those sealed Israelites is certainly an ideal number, that is to say, twelve times twelve thousand, or one hundred and forty-four thousand, a perfectly balanced number. But what makes them an 'ideal' Israel is not entirely their number, but, rather, their moral, religious qualities."

The Society calls the 144,000 "ideal Israel," so since twelve times 12,000 is an "ideal number," that "proves" they're the *Ideal Israel, Spiritual Israel,* made up, for the most part, of married Gentiles!

Then on page 35 they get deeper in "proving" their point—to the point of contradiction: "Natural, fleshly Israel was founded upon the twelve sons of the patriarch Jacob, but it is the spiritual Israel, the Christian Israel, that is founded on the twelve apostles of the Lamb Jesus Christ (Ephesians 2:20). So, without question, it is this spiritual Israel that is 'the ideal Israel.' "

By their own statement the 144,000 are fleshly Israel, literal descendants of the sons of Jacob, but they use it to prove that these are the 144,000 going to heaven, and that these are "spiritual Israel." The round-and-round illogic of the Watchtower Society is enough to make one dizzy, and I suppose that is by design. The average, intellectually honest person who reads the Watchtower reasoning might laugh it off. But the brainwashed multitude now numbers in the millions. These are people who had a void in their hearts for God, but it was filled instead by the Society. They wanted bread, but were given sawdust, and now they are full but not nourished. What may seem like a comedy is in reality a tragedy.

We find that there are Old Testament saints in

heaven: many would come from the east and the west and sit down with Abraham, Isaac, and Jacob in the kingdom of heaven. We find there are New Testament saints in heaven. In II Corinthians 5:8 the Apostle Paul spoke of being absent from the body and being present with the Lord. Where is the Lord? In heaven. And so when a Christian dies he is separated from his body and is present with the Lord immediately.

We find also that the saints who are still living when Jesus Christ comes back are going to heaven. In I Thessalonians 4:14-17 the Bible tells us that when the Lord Jesus Christ comes back, the dead in Christ are going to rise first, that is, be resurrected. "Then we which are alive and remain shall be caught up together with them in the clouds, to meet the Lord in the air: and so shall we ever be with the Lord." Those are the believers, the saints, who are living when Jesus Christ comes back. So we have Old Testament saints in the past in heaven, New Testament saints in heaven, and saints in the future who are going to rise with the Lord to heaven.

Though there are no classes of salvation, there is a difference in rewards. Every person who is now saved is going to heaven. One person might get more rewards for serving the Lord more, or being more faithful, doing more good works, but all of the saved of today are going to be in heaven. During the millennial kingdom of Christ and thereafter the earth will be populated by the survivors of the tribulation period over whom the believers of this age will rule, but this is another subject.

The Society teaches that you not only have to accept *The Truth,* every jot and tittle of their doctrines, but you've got to work, work, work. Every *publisher* is expected to turn in his report on how many hours he worked during the week. If he consistently fails to turn in a report he loses his status as a *publisher,* and is in danger of losing what credit he had earned toward salvation.

I put on the "Watchtower" bag and went out on the street to sell *The Watchtower.* I carried a satchel of books and went door to door trying to earn my salvation. We used what was called a "testimony card." When a person answered the door, I didn't have to say anything, just hand them the *testimony card.* The *testimony card* introduced me as "Joe Hewitt, an ordained minister of the gospel." To try to earn credit toward salvation, we tried to "place" booklets, *Watchtowers,* and books. We didn't "sell" them, we *placed* them. The difference was that we would "give" them to people, and then they in turn would give a "contribution." The reports we filled out included a record of each piece of material we left with people to whom we *witnessed.*

Usually we were furnished back copies of *The Watchtower* magazine to give away to interested people. Placing the old *Watchtower* copy was the lowest score we could make. Next higher was to *place* a booklet, then higher was to *place* a book, which was designed to indoctrinate the prospect into the Watchtower doctrines. Regarded even higher, though, was a subscription to *The Watchtower,* which brought the doctrines into the home on a regular basis. Anyone who subscribed was considered a prime prospect.

Each Witness bought and paid for his own supply of booklets and books from the *book servant* at the Kingdom Hall. I always paid the same price for them as the requested *contribution.* By buying in quantity, Witnesses could get a small discount. *Pioneers* who spent almost full time in the *witness work* received a sizeable discount. My stepfather, Ray, always bought in quantity, and placed many pieces of material. Often a Witness will give away booklets and the nominally priced books in order to make his report look better. It was not recorded on the report whether the prospect actually made a *contribution*. Therefore, in many cases the Witness was earnestly working to earn points toward salvation by going door to door and giving away printed material for which he had personally paid. It's almost as if he didn't realize that Jehovah knew how much time he spent, and how many books and subscriptions he placed, so he had to fill out the reports and send them through the proper channels.

When I first became a Witness we used an old windup phonograph. It was necessary to hold it up horizontally with one arm, lift the lid, place the needle on the record, switch it on, and hold it level while it played the short message by Judge Rutherford. Later, the Society developed a new model. It was about the size of an attache case, and was much easier to use. While holding it by the handle, we had to but pull a trigger, located directly under the carrying handle, and the phonograph would play its message while held in the vertical carrying position.

The first step at the door was to use the *testimony card* as an introduction, then to play the phonograph, usually on the doorstep; we didn't wait to be invited in. If we could progress that far, we then tried to place a *Watchtower* subscription, book or booklet.

If successful in placing literature we then tried to make arrangements for a *book study* in the person's home once a week. This was the crowning achievement, because it is through the *book studies* that most new Witnesses are recruited. I helped conduct book studies, and occasionally conducted them as a substitute, but usually the older, more experienced men conducted them.

If the person visited accepted some literature, we would make a notation by his name and address "B.C." and then fill out a *back call* slip, and long after finishing the *territory* and turning the territory card and map back in to the *territory servant* we would be making *back calls* in that territory. The weekly report had a place for *back calls* and *book studies* which greatly enhanced it and raised the prestige of the Witness making the report.

The hardest working Witness I ever knew was my stepfather. He *pioneered* for many years. And though he never seemed to have any difficulty in making a living, the *witness work* always came first, and he spent much more time at it than he did in secular work.

During one of our milder discussions, I asked Ray why he drove himself so, going door to door daily, and putting out *The Watchtower* on the street corners. He was getting old and needed to start letting up. He stressed the need to *remain faithful to the end.*

"Surely if anyone could earn his salvation, you could have done it in over thirty years of working for it. Ray, suppose you go haywire, and for a few days quit witnessing, go out and get drunk, and then die? Would all your work have been for nothing?" I asked.

"Yes," he answered solemnly.

I believe it is this anxiety that killed my mother. She feared that she couldn't *endure faithfully to the end,* and since she couldn't increase her own endurance, she hastened the end.

How is a sinner saved? A sinner is saved, the cultists say, through their organization exclusively. And the Jehovah's Witnesses say you can't make it to heaven anyway, but you might have eternal life on earth if you earn it. But the Bible says, "All have sinned, and come short of the glory of God . . ." for "As it is written, There is none righteous, no not one" (Romans 3:23, 10). There is no classification of sinners, some being eligible for heaven and some not. Romans 10:9 is addressed to all: Believe in your heart that Jesus Christ is Lord, and you will be saved. That salvation is a gift. "For the wages of sin is death, but the gift of God is eternal life through Jesus Christ our Lord" (Romans 6:23).

Ephesians 2:8-9: "For by grace are ye saved through faith; and that not of yourselves: it is the gift of God: Not of works, lest any man should boast." All the years I was growing up as a brainwashed servant of the Watchtower Society, I never heard that verse preached, nor read about that verse in any of the Watchtower literature.

Salvation is a gift; it is completely by the grace of God. Grace is the free unmerited favor of God. If anything is added to grace that one must do before he can receive grace, then it's not grace.

The Apostle Paul made this clear in Romans 11:6: "And if by grace, then is it no more of works: otherwise grace is no more grace. But if it be of works, then is it no more grace: otherwise work is no more work." It's one or the other. It's either works or grace, and if anything is added to grace it's not grace anymore.

So where then does that believer go when he dies? The Witnesses believe that when a person dies he is dead like a dog and is without conscious existence until the resurrection. Then he is tried by God who decides whether he gets to live eternally on the earth, or is to die the second death. But what does the Bible say?

The Bible says that the believer goes to heaven. Matthew 6:20 says, "But lay up for yourselves treasures in heaven, where neither moth nor rust doth corrupt, and where thieves do not break through nor steal." The believer can have treasures in heaven. The Bible tells us that our names are written in heaven. Luke 10:20: "Notwithstanding in this rejoice not, that the spirits are subject unto you; but rather rejoice, because your names are written in heaven." The believer has an eternal home in heaven.

II Corinthians 5:1 says, "For we know that if our earthly house of this tabernacle were dissolved, we have a building of God, an house not made with hands, eternal in the heavens."

The Society says these scriptures mean only *the elect*, but all believers are of the elect. The Society, not the Bible, divides believers into *the elect* and the non-elect.

The heavenly Jerusalem is in heaven, not on earth; it comes down from heaven as John saw in his vision (Revelation 21:2). But it is still the heavenly city, the heavenly Jerusalem; the Scripture does not say it actually rests on the earth, nor does the Scripture preclude the possibility that it will rise again into heaven. Hebrews 12:22 says, "But ye are come unto mount Sion, and unto the city of the living God, the heavenly Jerusalem, and to an innumerable company of angels." The believer is going to heaven.

Witnesses think they will be resurrected and populate the earth. The Bible says that the children of the resurrection do not marry. Luke 20:35-36: "But they which shall be accounted worthy to obtain that world, and the resurrection from the dead, neither marry, nor are given in marriage: Neither can they die any more: for they are equal unto the angels; and are the children of God, being the children of the resurrection." Resurrected believers go to heaven (I Thessalonians 4:17).

To find the many things that shoot the Watchtower doctrines full of holes, just read the Bible. The Bible tells us that to be absent from the body is to be present with the Lord (II Corinthians 5:8). The cultists say you must affiliate with their organization to be saved. The Bible doesn't teach that at all, but rather that salvation is a very personal thing. Believe on the Lord Jesus Christ and *thou* shalt be saved. God loved you as an individual, and Christ died for you, an individual, because He loved you. Trust Him.

13
Transfusion: "Don't Eat the Blood"

During a visit with my mother many years ago, the conversation got around to accidents. She removed a card from her purse and said, "If I am ever in an accident, and can't speak for myself, don't ever let them give me a blood transfusion. This card says it's against my religion."

August 11, 1968, 22-year-old Robert Pelzek of Oak Creek, Minnesota, crashed his car off a highway near Racine, Wisconsin. He suffered a skull fracture and broken collar bone, and was taken to St. Luke's Hospital in Racine, where doctors said he was recovering well. But due to the stress of the accident and injuries, Pelzek developed a stomach ulcer, making blood transfusions necessary.

Pelzek, who had been raised a Catholic, had just two years before married a young woman who converted him to become a Jehovah's Witness.

Because of his religious beliefs, Pelzek refused to take the necessary blood transfusions. The doctor warned him that he would die if he continued to refuse. Several hours later he was dead (UPI report in *Dallas Morning News*).

In the spring of 1970, Mr. and Mrs. Robert Johnson of Athol, Massachusetts, were told their 5-year-old son, Terry, needed open heart surgery. A congenital heart defect caused him to be always short of breath and exhausted, and he probably would not live many more years because of it. The doctors were 90 percent sure that the operation would make him well, but his parents refused to allow it because blood transfusions would be necessary, a violation of their religious beliefs as Jehovah's Witnesses.

The doctors suggested removing some of Terry's own blood over a period of time, and using it during the surgery, but the parents refused. The doctors considered seeking a court order, but the parents said that if the transfusions were performed they would not take Terry back into their home. Because of the ingenuity of the doctors, the surgery was performed successfully without blood transfusions (*Newsweek*).

Why would people be willing to die rather than to take a blood transfusion? Why would parents be willing to let their own child die? Why would parents be more willing to abandon their child than to accept him back into their home after having taken a blood transfusion? The answer is: the Watchtower Society teaches that taking a blood transfusion is the same as eating blood, and they believe that the observance of Old Testament law against eating blood is necessary for salvation.

Many people today, especially in Europe, eat blood sausage, and blood pudding, thinking nothing of it because they believe the Old Testament dietary laws are no longer in effect. I don't need any kind of law to keep me from eating blood, a sentiment that I believe is shared by most Americans. But at the same time I know the difference between eating and intravenous injection. Even if the Old Testament dietary law were still in effect, it would not prohibit blood transfusions, but let's examine the scriptures the Society uses to promulgate this doctrine, and the iron discipline that has caused people to die, rather than transgress.

Without a doubt, the Old Testament law was against eating blood. Genesis 9:4: "But flesh with the life thereof, which is the blood thereof, shall ye not eat." To make this mean a prohibition of blood transfusions is using the same kind of Pharisaical progression of cumulative legalisms as that which has resulted in the modern Orthodox Jew's refusal to eat meat and dairy products at the same meal, or even from the same plate at different meals.

The Orthodox Jewish doctrine is based on the commands in Exodus 23:19, ". . . Thou shalt not seethe a kid in his mother's milk." (See also Exodus 34:26 and Deuteronomy 14:21.) A pagan fertility rite involved boiling a kid sheep or goat in its mother's milk, then sprinkling the broth over the flocks and fields. God's people were not to participate.

Those Hebrews who delighted in adding to the law decided that it would be better not to boil a kid in any milk, lest perchance it be the mother's. The next step was not to eat any meat at the same meal at which milk was served. Later that was expanded to include any dairy product. The law continued to be added to until a piece of cheese or any dairy product could not be placed on the same plate on which meat had been eaten, lest the commandment be violated. This hyperlegalism necessitates two complete sets of dishes for the strict Orthodox Jewish family.

The Society has similarly added to the prohibition against eating blood to the point that they refuse to take an innoculation against disease that involves blood serum, and to the point of letting their children die rather than take a blood transfusion.

The Society claims that the Old Testament law against eating blood was continued in the New Testament in Acts 15:20, "But that we write unto them, that they abstain from pollutions of idols, and from fornication, and from things strangled, and from blood." This scripture has been lifted out of context and wrapped in a false meaning. Let's examine it in context.

In the first of the chapter, we see that the Judaizers were adding to the gospel and confusing the new Gentile believers by saying they had to be circumcised to be saved. Paul and Barnabas, of course, disputed this false doctrine, and it was agreed to take the question to the apostles at Jerusalem. There, the people with a Pharisee background echoed the Judaizers position, but Peter said, "Why tempt ye God, to put a yoke upon the neck of the disciples, which neither our fathers nor we were able to bear? But we believe that through the grace of the Lord Jesus Christ we shall be saved, even as they" (Acts 15:10-11). Peter recognized that the Gentile believers were saved.

James, who apparently was the pastor, or spokesman for the apostles said, "My sentence is, that we trouble not them, which from among the Gentiles are turned to God: But that we write unto them, that they abstain from pollutions of idols, and from fornication, and from things strangled, and from blood" (verses 19-20).

Why? Were these the only sins the Gentile believers could commit? Were they free to murder, steal, and lie? Why did James mention only abstaining from eating food that had been offered to idols, from the fornication that was so common in the Greek cities of the day, from eating meat from animals that had been strangled, and from eating blood?

The reason is given in the very next verse: "For Moses of old time hath in every city them that preach him, being read in the synagogues every sabbath day" (verse 21). James had not listed the "works" by which the Gentiles could be saved; he listed the things the Gentile believers specifically should not do in order to keep from offending the Jews! The very reason for the Jerusalem meeting was to demonstrate that the believer does not have to add works to the grace of God in order to be saved. But the Society lifts one verse out of context to prove the opposite!

Let's examine one of the other admonitions James gave in his decision concerning the Gentiles: "Abstain from pollutions of idols." This was the same problem that Paul discussed in Romans 14, and I Corinthians 10. In both these chapters, it is clearly established that there was no sin, per se, in eating meat that had been sacrificed to idols, but if such eating were part of pagan worship it would be wrong, or if such eating caused a brother to be offended it would be wrong. The latter is exactly why James included it in his message to the Gentile believers; and it is exactly why he included "from blood" (Acts 15:19-29).

The Society would have Peter saying, "You don't have to be circumcised to be saved," and then they would have James say, "But you do have to observe certain dietary laws to be saved." Peter and James did not contradict each other. And the Bible does not contradict itself. Grace is still grace, and works is still works: And if by grace, then is it no more of works: . . . But if it be of works, then is it no more grace . . ." (Romans 11:6).

Christians have long been accused of having a preoccupation with blood. In the early days they were accused of being cannibals by pagans who did not understand the Lord's Supper. Today, Christians who preach the atonement of Christ, stress His shed blood: ". . . which he hath purchased with his own blood . . ." (Acts 20:28). "In whom we have redemption through his blood, the forgiveness of sins, according to the riches of his grace" (Ephesians 1:7). "How much more shall the blood of Christ, who through the eternal Spirit offered himself without spot to God, purge your conscience from dead works to serve the living God?" (Hebrews 9:14). The blood of Jesus Christ being shed for us is an essential part of the gospel story, ". . . the blood of Jesus Christ his Son cleanseth us from all sin" (I John 1:7).

But some of the cults' emphasis is not on the blood of Christ. For example, the Mormons believe that man's shedding his own blood can atone for his sins. The Watchtower Society is preoccupied with blood generally, but not Christ's shed blood. In their book, *Life Everlasting in Freedom of the Sons of God,* which contained the chart indicating that Armageddon would occur in the Autumn of 1975, there are several odd references to blood. They note such "milestones" of history as:

1492 Pope Innocent VIII dies after blood transfusion.

1918 First use of stored blood . . .

1937 First blood bank on a large scale established at Cook County Hospital.

1945 Watchtower exposes blood transfusion, Psalm 16:4.

1963 Pope John XIII . . . dies despite blood transfusions.

It is as if the Watchtower just discovered Psalm 16:4 in 1945. It is a Psalm of David: "Their sorrows shall be multiplied that hasten after another god: their drink offerings of blood will I not offer, nor take up their names into my lips."

There's only one group that I know of that claims to be Christian that believes in two gods, and that's the Jehovah's Witnesses. They believe that Jehovah is the Creator, and that He created Jesus, the Christ, a lesser god, and then commissioned Christ to create everything else.

David was talking about people that hasten after another god. He said, "their drink offerings of blood will I not offer." He did not mention eating blood. The worshipers of Jehovah in the Old Testament offered a drink offering of wine; they offered an offering of meal, and an offering of oil, but the pagans offered a drink offering of blood. David was not talking about taking blood transfusions, nor was he talking about eating blood. This is another case of the Society taking a verse of scripture out of context and putting a different meaning on it to suit its own purposes.

The Pharisees sought to kill Jesus because they believed He violated the Sabbath by healing on that day. This is the same reasoning that would cause a parent to kill his own child by denying him proper medical treatment; he would kill the child rather than violate his man-made Pharisaical doctrine.

14
Does Jesus Christ Make Two Gods?

"Jehovah's Witnesses" claim to be Christians, yet the central doctrine of Christianity is Christ, whose deity they deny.

"Christ" from the Greek language, and "Messiah" from the Hebrew language, mean the same thing: "the Anointed One." He was promised to come and be our Saviour, to be Immanuel, which means "God with us," or "God in the flesh." Christ claimed to be that promised Messiah (John 4:26). He said He was one with the Father (John 10:30). *Yet the Watchtower Society denies that Jesus Christ is anything more than a created being.* The Watchtower book *Then is Finished the Mystery of God,* says on page 249 that Jesus Christ was, before his human birth, the Archangel Michael. This would rank Him with Lucifer. They deny that Christ is eternal, without beginning and without end. That makes the Watchtower religion not a Christian religion.

One of the first doctrines concerning Himself that Almighty God taught His people Israel, was that He is One God, and that He would tolerate no other gods before, or in addition to Himself (Deuteronomy 6:4; Exodus 20:3). Therefore, when the prophets speak of God or the LORD, they are speaking of Jehovah, the Self-Existent One, the LORD of Creation, the Great First Cause of all things.

Examine Isaiah 9:6, a prophecy of Christ, "For unto us a child is born, unto us a son is given: and the government shall be upon his shoulder: and his name shall be called Wonderful, Counsellor, The mighty

God, The everlasting Father, The Prince of Peace."
The Prophet Isaiah, speaking more than 700 years
before the birth of Christ, was speaking of one who
would be born, who would be a son, who would
receive the government, who would be the Wonderful
Counselor, with whom we could have a personal relationship; He would be one and the same Everlasting
Father, and be one and the same Prince of Peace.
This is a description of Jesus Christ, the eternal Son
of God.

Part of that prophecy has been fulfilled. Christ was
born in Bethlehem. He, the Son of God, was given as
a sacrifice for our sins. According to Bible prophecy
the government shall be upon His shoulder when He
returns to earth to rule and reign in righteousness.
He is now the Wonderful Counselor to those who
know Him personally as Lord and Saviour, and will
be more so known when He personally rules from the
throne of David in Jerusalem. He is the mighty God,
not *a* god, but *the* God. He is the everlasting Father.
He is the Prince of Peace.

The same prophet said in Isaiah 7:14, "Therefore
the Lord himself shall give you a sign; Behold, a
virgin shall conceive, and bear a son, and shall call
his name Immanuel."

The birth of Jesus was proclaimed by the angel of
the Lord in Matthew 1:22-23 to be the fulfillment of
that prophecy: "Now all this was done, that it might
be fulfilled which was spoken of the Lord by the prophet, saying, Behold, a virgin shall be with child, and
shall bring forth a son, and they shall call his name
Emmanuel, which being interpreted is, God with us."
Jesus Christ, born of the Virgin Mary, was Emmanuel, God with us, God in the flesh. Remember
that "the Lord he is God; there is none else beside
him" Deuteronomy 4:35; see also Deuteronomy 6:4;
32:39; II Samuel 7:22; I Chronicles 17:20; Psalm
83:18; 86:10; Isaiah 43:10; 44:6; 45:18; Mark 12:29; I

Corinthians 8:4; Ephesians 4:6; I Timothy 2:5; I John 5:7).

Another prophecy concerning the coming Christ was made by the Prophet Micah, a contemporary of Isaiah. He said in Micah 5:2, "But thou, Bethlehem Ephratah, though thou be little among the thousands of Judah, yet out of thee shall he come forth unto me that is to be ruler in Israel; whose goings forth have been from of old, from everlasting." A believer could see from this: Christ would be born in Bethlehem. He could also see from this: Christ had no beginning; He was from everlasting. Michael the archangel had a beginning; he was not from everlasting. Only the LORD is eternal without a beginning.

The Bible makes it plain that only Jehovah God the LORD, is our Saviour. "I, even I, am the LORD; and beside me there is no saviour" (Isaiah 43:11). The Witnesses call Jesus Christ, our "Lord and Saviour." If the Society's teachings were true, they would be insulting Jehovah by calling Jesus "Saviour." The LORD is one God; He will tolerate no other gods beside Him; He is our only Saviour: Therefore Jesus and Jehovah are one, yet we know from God's Word that they are two distinct persons. Mary, the virgin, whom God used to bring forth His Son, Jesus, praised God and said, "And my spirit hath rejoiced in God my Saviour" (Luke 1:47). The LORD came to earth in the person of Jesus Christ our Lord and Saviour: ". . . this is indeed the Christ, the Saviour of the world" (John 4:42). Throughout the Old Testament, God's Word teaches that only the LORD (Jehovah) is the Saviour. In the New Testament the Lord Jesus Christ, and God, are called Saviour, and they are one.

"They forgat God their saviour . . ." (Psalm 106:21).

"Verily thou art a God that hidest thyself, O God

of Israel, the Saviour" (Isaiah 45:15).

". . . who hath declared this from ancient time? who hath told it from that time? have not I the LORD? and there is no God else beside me; a just God and a Saviour; there is none beside me" (Isaiah 45:21). A belief in a secondary, lesser god as Saviour, would be in direct contradiction to this scripture. The only way this scripture can harmonize with the New Testament is that the LORD Jehovah and the Lord Jesus Christ are One.

There are many others that bring us to the same conclusion. For example Isaiah 45:22-23, "Look unto me, and be ye saved, all the ends of the earth: for I am God, and there is none else. I have sworn by myself, the word is gone out of my mouth in righteousness, and shall not return, That unto me every knee shall bow, every tongue shall swear." The Apostle Paul was referring back to Isaiah 45:23 in Romans 14:10,11: ". . . for we shall all stand before the judgment seat of Christ. For it is written, As I live, saith the Lord, every knee shall bow to me, and every tongue shall confess to God."

Then again in Philippians 2:9-12 the same Old Testament scripture is alluded to when Paul said, "Wherefore God also hath highly exalted him, and given him a name which is above every name: That at the name of Jesus every knee should bow, of things in heaven, and things in earth, and things under the earth; And that every tongue should confess that Jesus Christ is Lord, to the glory of God the Father." The Greek word "Kurios" translated "Lord" here is the same word the Watchtower translates "Jehovah" in Romans 14:11.

Instead of changing their doctrines to fit the Bible, the Watchtower changed their bible to fit their doctrine.

". . . I the LORD am thy Saviour and thy Redeemer . . ." (Isaiah 49:26).

"... I the LORD am thy Saviour and thy Redeemer, the mighty One of Jacob" (Isaiah 60:16).

These scriptures establish beyond a doubt that the LORD (Jehovah) is the only Saviour and Redeemer. Yet the New Testament clearly states that Jesus Christ is our Saviour:

"For unto you is born this day in the city of David a Saviour, which is Christ the Lord" (Luke 2:11).

"Him hath God exalted with his right hand to be a Prince and a Saviour, for to give repentance to Israel, and forgiveness of sins" (Acts 5:31).

"For our conversation is in heaven; from whence also we look for the Saviour, the Lord Jesus Christ" (Philippians 3:20).

The Apostle Paul, who so often referred to Jesus as Lord and Saviour, in I Timothy 1:1 said, "... by the commandment of God our Saviour, and Lord Jesus Christ, which is our hope." Again in I Timothy 2:3, he said, "For this is good and acceptable in the sight of God our Saviour ...." "... according to the commandment of God our Saviour; To Titus, mine own son after the common faith: Grace, mercy, and peace, from God the Father and the Lord Jesus Christ our Saviour" (Titus 1:3-4; see also Titus 2:10, 13, and 3:4, 6).

The Apostle Peter also made many references to Jesus Christ as Lord and Saviour: "Simon Peter, a servant and an apostle of Jesus Christ, to them that have obtained like precious faith with us through the righteousness of God and our Saviour Jesus Christ: ... into the everlasting kingdom of our Lord and Saviour Jesus Christ. ... through the knowledge of the Lord and Saviour Jesus Christ ... That ye may be mindful of the words which were spoken before by the holy prophets, and of the commandment of us the apostles of the Lord and Saviour ... But grow in grace, and in the knowledge of our Lord and Saviour Jesus Christ. To him be glory both now and for ever.

Amen" (II Peter 1:1, 11; 2:20; 3:2,18).

The Apostle John, who so clearly stated that Christ was the eternal God, without beginning, in John 1:1-3, said in I John 4:14, "And we have seen and do testify that the Father sent the Son to be the Saviour of the world."

It is difficult for the human mind to understand how that God was in Heaven in the person of the Father, and on earth in the person of the Son at the same time. Many times I have seen two or three Witnesses brag to each other about how they got the best of some *goat* in an argument by saying, "Who ran the universe for three days and nights while Jesus was in the grave?" Whereupon his admiring audience would laugh. Ridicule of non-witnesses is an integral part of the Watchtower culture.

The Watchtower book *Let God Be True* says ". . . Who ran the universe during the three days that Jesus was in the grave, or, for that matter, during the thirty-three and a half years on the earth while he was made a 'little lower than the angels'?"

Colossians 1:16-17 says Jesus created all things and ". . . by him all things consist." He is holding the universe together. The Society's idea of God is just not big enough for One who could be in heaven as the Father, on both earth and in heaven as the Holy Spirit, and incarnate and in humility on earth as the Son, all at the same time, and yet be One God, omnipresent and omnipotent. To doubt Bible truth for that reason is to put limits on God. Just because *we* can't do or even imagine such a thing doesn't mean God can't. God has no limits.

Jesus Himself said in John 3:13, "And no man hath ascended up to heaven, but he that came down from heaven, even the Son of man which is in heaven." Jesus was standing on earth, speaking to Nicodemus. But *He was also in heaven at the same time.* The Watchtower's Greek-English New Testament says, "And no one has ascended into the heaven, except he out of the heaven having descended, the son of the man, (the being in the heaven)."

Christ has many names and titles, among these is the "Word." The Watchtower people agree with all Bible scholars that the "Word" spoken of in John 1:1 is Christ: "In the beginning was the Word, and the Word was with God, and the Word was God. The same was in the beginning with God. All things were made by him; and without him was not any thing made that was made" (John 1:1-3).

You don't have to be a Bible scholar to understand what the Word of God plainly says. In the beginning Christ already existed. He already existed and was with God. Christ was God, and He always was God. And just to make sure we don't misunderstand, the Apostle John repeated: "The same was in the beginning with God." He, Christ, made everything that was made. He did not make Himself.

These and other scriptures that so plainly refute the Watchtower doctrines became such a thorn in the Society's side that they had to write their own Bible. In this text of Scripture, the Watchtower has inserted the article "a" before "God" and made it to read: "In (the) beginning the Word was, and the Word was with God, and the Word was a god."

One lie leads to another, so this made the brainwashed multitude believe in *two Gods*, Jehovah and Jesus. This is a violation of God's clear command in Exodus 20:3, "Thou shalt have no other gods before me." It is a clear contradiction to Deuteronomy 6:4, "Hear, O Israel: The LORD our God is one LORD." But the disciplined Witness doesn't allow these scriptures and his own arguments against *Christendom's three gods* logic to cross over the partition in his swept and garnished mind to the compartment that claims Christ is another god. To do so would cause a neurological short circuit.

Jesus was either the promised Messiah, the promised Immanuel, or He lied when he said in John 4:26, "... I that speak unto thee am he [the Messiah]."

Almighty God, in proclaiming His Name to Moses said, "I AM" (Exodus 3:14). Jesus proclaimed Himself to be that same I AM. "Jesus said unto them, Verily, verily, I say unto you, Before Abraham was, I am" (John 8:58). The Jews took up stones to stone Him. Why? Because Jesus had proclaimed Himself to be the Great I AM, The LORD, Jehovah, the Self-Existent One. The Watchtower Society does the same thing today; they try to "stone" Him for the same reason.

Charles Taze Russell, founder of the Watch Tower, couldn't understand how that Jehovah as Christ could come to earth in humility and under subjection of the Father. Russell, and his spiritual descendants, limited God.

Jehovah's ability to be one God, yet to be manifest to us in more than one person at the same time, is also denied by the Watchtower Society on the basis of rationalism. The same rationale should apply to Luke 2:51 which says Jesus, as a child, was subject to Mary and Joseph.

"And he went down with them, and came to Nazareth, and was subject unto them ... And Jesus increased in wisdom and stature, and in favour with God and man" (Luke 2:51-52).

If a created, lesser god, could lay aside the free exercise of his power, humble himself and be obedient to earthly parents, and later reclaim his power and glory, why couldn't the Almighty God do the same thing in the person of His Son?

If Jesus had come to earth in all His glory and power, His admonitions to us to pray, to have faith, and to completely trust God, would have been without personal example. When Jesus told His disciples to pray, He also demonstrated prayer and faith. He had left the free exercise of His power in Heaven and trusted in the Father and the Holy Spirit, exercising faith as an example to us.

An example of this humility before the Father is found in John 10:27-30: "My sheep hear my voice, and I know them, and they follow me: And I give unto them eternal life; and they shall never perish, neither shall any man pluck them out of my hand. My father, which gave them me, is greater than all; and no man is able to pluck them out of my Father's hand. I and my Father are one."

I have heard His voice, and followed Jesus. According to this scripture He has given to me eternal life. I am in His hand, and no man can pluck me out of His hand. I am also in the Father's hand. This presents a problem, if according to the Watchtower doctrine, the Father and Son are two separate gods. To be consistent with their simplistic rationalism, I would have to become two persons, one of me in the Son's hand and the other of me in the Father's. But these scriptures are no problem at all if we believe the Bible, that the Father and Son are one.

Hebrews 1:3 likens Christ's relationship to the Father to light's relationship to the sun: inseparable. This verse also tells us that after Christ had purged sin by His sacrificial death for the sinner, he regained his heavenly glory. Much of the book of Hebrews is directed toward explaining the greatness of Christ in eternity past and eternity future.

It was necessary for Christ to humble Himself and become a man in order to be the propitiation, or sacrificial offering, for our sins, which humbling of Himself the Watchtower Society believes that Jehovah God could not do.

Believers in New Testament times ascribed the same glory to Christ as God: for example, "... To him be glory both now and for ever. Amen" (II Peter

3:18), Peter wrote to the Christians in Pontus and Bithynia. Pliney the Younger (Gaius Plinius Caecilius Secundus), proconsul of Pontus and Bithynia, and persecutor of the Christians there, wrote to the Roman Emperor, Trajan, and said the Christians were wont to address hymns to Christ as to God.

In hymns, in prayers, and doxologies, God and Christ are addressed as one: "I give thee charge in the sight of God, who quickeneth all things, and before Christ Jesus ... That thou keep this commandment without spot, unrebukeable, until the appearing of our Lord Jesus Christ: Which in his times he shall shew, who is the blessed and only Potentate, the King of kings, and Lord of lords; Who only hath immortality, dwelling in the light which no man can approach unto; whom no man hath seen, nor can see: to whom be honour and power everlasting. Amen" (I Timothy 6:13-16). If Jesus were not one with the Father, He could not be "the only Potentate, King of kings, and Lord of lords." The LORD our God, who is a jealous God, would not allow a lesser god to share in the "light which no man can approach unto; whom no man hath seen, nor can see."

Peter spoke in the same manner, glorifying God and Christ as one: ". . . that God in all things may be glorified through Jesus Christ, to whom be praise and dominion for ever and ever. Amen" (I Peter 4:11).

Likewise John wrote: ". . . Worthy is the Lamb that was slain to receive power, and riches, and wisdom, and strength, and honour, and glory, and blessing. And every creature which is in heaven, and on the earth, and under the earth, and such as are in the sea, and all that are in them, heard I saying, Blessing, and honour, and glory, and power, be unto him that sitteth upon the throne, and unto the Lamb for ever and ever" (Revelation 5:12-13).

Another example of a blatant, dishonest, attempt

to change the meaning of scripture to fit their doctrines is in the NWT's John 14:8-9. The King James Version says, "Philip saith unto him, Lord, shew us the Father, and it sufficeth us. Jesus saith unto him, Have I been so long time with you, and yet hast thou not known me, Philip? he that hath seen me hath seen the Father; and how sayest thou then, Shew us the Father?" The NWT says, "Philip said to him: 'Lord, show us the Father, and it is enough for us.' Jesus said to him: 'Have I been with you men so long a time, and yet, Philip, you have not come to know me? He that has seen me has seen the Father [also]. How is it you say 'Show us the Father'?" By inserting the word "also" in brackets the meaning is destroyed. But then that was the Watchtower Society's purpose in inserting the word without any basis whatever except to make it fit their doctrine.

The Watchtower Society uses some of the same methods as the communists: whenever they are guilty of wrong, and even vulnerable to being exposed for it, they draw attention away from it by accusing their opponents of being guilty of it. For example, Red Russia is continuing to promulgate the imperialistic goals of Peter the Great, and are openly trying to take over the world, so they accuse the West of being "imperialistic." The communists have a totalitarian society with little personal freedom, yet they call their attempts at conquest "liberation movements."

Although many things that the Watchtower teaches are true, their distinctive doctrines are obviously homemade, and vulnerable to exposure. So the Society charges orthodox Christianity with "teaching the doctrines of men instead of the doctrines of God." We should heed the warning in Colossians 2:8-9, "Beware lest any man spoil you through philosophy and vain deceit, after the tradition of men, after the rudiments of the world, and not after

Christ." The Society tries to accomplish that deceit by denying the truth in the following verse, "For in him dwelleth all the fulness of the Godhead bodily."

The Book of Revelation is the revelation of Jesus Christ, which God gave unto Him and which was given by His angel to John, who gave it to us (Revelation 1:1). Words of Christ in first person could sometimes be spoken by Christ, the Father, or the Holy Spirit. "Behold, he cometh with clouds; and every eye shall see him, and they also which pierced him: and all kindreds of the earth shall wail because of him. Even so, Amen. I am Alpha and Omega, the beginning and the ending, saith the Lord, which is, and which was, and which is to come, the Almighty" (Revelation 1:7-8). Christ certainly is the one who was pierced, the one that will come in the clouds, and He is also the Alpha and Omega.

The letter to the church at Pergamos (2:12-17) is clearly from Jesus, yet He says "He that hath an ear, let him hear what the Spirit saith unto the churches . . ." (Revelation 2:17).

The New Testament clearly teaches that the Messiah is God come in the flesh. Judaism rejects that teaching, but does not at the same time claim to be Christian. The Watchtower Society rejects that teaching, but still claims to be Christian, when in reality, their religion is more akin to Judaism than to Christianity. But Judaism certainly wouldn't claim any kinship with them, because the Witnesses believe in two gods, an embarrassing situation forced upon them by their denial of the deity of Jesus Christ.

The Society's "Watchtower" is built upon a crooked foundation, the denial that Jesus Christ is God. As they laid good, square stone upon this uneven foundation, their tower began to lean, so they had to lay another uneven stone to compensate, and that was the doctrine that Jesus Christ was *a god.* That stone was even more wedge-shaped than the original error in their foundation. They can lay many other truthful doctrines on top of that wedge-shaped heresy, but the tower is still not straight, it is still leaning, though in the other direction, and the Society is compelled to periodically come up with *New Light* to keep it from toppling.

15
What Is God's Name?

It is not necessary, by any means, to be a linguist in order to understand the Bible. God gave us the Bible so we could learn how we got in the shape we're in, and how, by His grace, we can get out of it. Any person can take any honest translation of the Bible, and learn that he is a sinner, needs a Saviour, and that God loves him and provided a way through Jesus Christ for him to receive pardon.

Even though before my salvation I had believed the Watchtower doctrines, when I received Christ as my Lord and Saviour, I did not think of Him as a second, lesser god. Jesus Christ, God the Father, and God the Holy Spirit, were somehow intermingled in my understanding. I couldn't explain it then, nor can most people who yield themselves to Jesus as LORD. The LORD our God is "a jealous God" (Exodus 20:5). He is One LORD (Deuteronomy 6:4). And He is the same LORD in Old Testament and New Testament. By simply reading the Bible in our native tongue, we understand the truth without having to hop back and forth from one language to the other. In this chapter, I am referring to these names and titles in Hebrew and Greek, not because it is necessary for the average person to understand it, but because of the verbal gymnastics practiced by the Watchtower Society to confuse the truth, which need to be corrected.

What is God's name? The answer is in Exodus 3:13-15. "And Moses said unto God, Behold, when I come unto the children of Israel, and shall say unto them, The God of your fathers hath sent me unto you; and they shall say to me, What is his name?

what shall I say unto them? And God said unto Moses, I AM THAT I AM: and he said, Thus shalt thou say unto the children of Israel, I AM hath sent me unto you. And God said moreover unto Moses, Thus shalt thou say unto the children of Israel, the LORD God of your fathers, the God of Abraham, the God of Isaac, and the God of Jacob, hath sent me unto you."

Moses was negotiating with God about going back to Egypt to lead the children of Israel out of bondage. Moses was negotiating, but God wasn't. God had already chosen Moses. Moses made the excuse that he wasn't eloquent. Then Moses questioned how he would explain who had sent him. The Egyptians had names for all their gods, but Moses had not heard a name for his God. Neither have you. And neither have I. Because the names used for God were all titles. For example, "El" in the Hebrew simply meant "The High;" "Shaddai" meant "The Strong;" and "Jehovah" meant "The Self-Existent One;" so we have no real names for God but titles. Jehovah's Witnesses teach that when you pray, if you don't use the Hebrew name for God, "Jehovah," your prayer might go to the wrong place, to the wrong person. Your prayers might go to the god of this world, Satan. It's hard to believe that grown-up, intelligent human beings could believe such a thing, but they do. And they teach it.

Imagine a father conversing with his little two-year-old son. The little son says to the father, "Da-da."

And the father says, "If you can't pronounce my name, 'Joseph,' in Hebrew, I'm not going to listen to you."

It doesn't make a lot of sense, does it? God does not operate that way. God has perfect hearing. And God is not tricky. He doesn't require that we pronounce the right formula in a particular language. He won't re-route our call to Satan!

The words we use to designate "the God" are titles. They are very much like earthly titles we use for our earthly fathers. My son, Gary, has never called me Joe. My name is Joe, but my kids call me Daddy.

Sometimes Deborah Ruth, our four-year-old grand-daughter, calls her grandmother, "Mama." Marylou says, "No, my name is 'Grandma.' " That's not her name. To me her name is "Marylou;" to our children it is "Mama," or "Mother," depending on the mood, but to Deborah Ruth it's "Grandma."

When Moses came to the LORD he asked His name, "Who shall I say sent me?" And the Lord said, "I AM THAT I AM." "I AM" means the One without any beginning, the One without any ending. "I AM" is a title. Then He identified Himself as the LORD God of your fathers, the God of Abraham, Isaac, and Jacob. He said, "this is my name forever." In the original, what is translated "LORD" was a tetragrammaton, a four-letter symbol roughly equivalent to "YHVH" or "YHWH." The English translators tried to make that symbol pro-nounceable. Some of the translators added English vowels and called it "Yahwe." Others added vowels and used the letter "J" instead of "Y" and spelled out the word "Jehovah." This is the most common.

YHVH is almost identical in meaning to what was translated, "I AM," and God Himself used these two names synonymously. "The Self Existent One" is a title. Like Marylou says to Deborah Ruth, "My name is Grandma," (which is a title), God says, "The LORD, the Self Existent One, the great I AM," is His name forever.

YHVH, the Self Existent One, is translated "LORD." And it's a good translation.

We don't have to talk to God in Hebrew. God understands English perfectly well. Otherwise, instead of saying "God," we would say "Elohim," which is the Hebrew word translated "God." But we speak English, so we say "God." Certainly we can say "Jehovah" if we want; God still understands. We can also call Jesus by His Hebrew name, "Joshua," if we want; He still understands. If the Watchtower Society were consistent, since they insist on using the Hebrew from the Old Testament for LORD, "Jehovah," they would use the Greek from the New Testament for Lord, "Kurios." And why don't they say "Theos" (Greek for "God") instead of God? We can say Jehovah; we can say God; we can say Lord. If we speak English, God can certainly understand us. He doesn't say, "Oh, you didn't say it right, so I'm going to send your prayer to Satan."

"I AM" could also have been translated "I Will Be that I Will Be." This "I AM" came in the flesh. John 4:25-26 records a conversation between Jesus and the Samaritan Woman: "The woman saith unto him, I know that Messias cometh, which is called Christ: when he is come, he will tell us all things. Jesus saith unto her, I that speak unto thee am *he*." Notice that in the King James Version of the Bible the word "he" is italicized, meaning that the word was not in the original. Jesus said, "I that speak unto thee AM." He was the same One that spoke to Moses out of the burning bush, the "I AM."

In John 10:30, Jesus said, "I and my Father are one." And the Jews took up stones to stone Him. Why? "Because that thou, being a man, makest thyself God," the Jews said (John 10:33). Today's Witnesses agree more with those Jews than they do with Jesus.

John 8:58: "Jesus said unto them, Verily, verily, I say unto you, Before Abraham was, I am." The Jews once again took up stones to stone Him for the same reason, because He had proclaimed that He was God in the flesh. He proclaimed that He was the fulfillment of the prophecy made in Isaiah 7:14, "Therefore the Lord himself shall give you a sign; Behold, a virgin shall conceive, and bear a son, and shall call his name Immanuel." Immanuel means "God with us," or "God in the flesh." Jesus claimed to be that promised Messiah, *I AM* in the flesh; not another god, but *the God*, in the flesh.

Isaiah 9:6 speaks of Christ: "Unto us a child is born, unto us a son is given," being the same as the "Wonderful, Counsellor, The mighty God, The everlasting Father, The Prince of Peace." God is not divisible. He is one God. But unto us a child is born. That one God, Immanuel, God with us, came in the flesh. His name is many great titles, including "Wonderful, Counsellor," but God is still one God.

In the Old Testament we see that God would come in the flesh. Then in the New Testament Jesus Christ claims to be that God in the flesh. The Septuagint, the 250 B.C. translation of the Hebrew Scriptures into Greek, uses for the word YHVH or LORD the Greek word "Kurios." Again and again in the New Testament when it speaks of the LORD God of the Old Testament it is rendered "Kurios" in the Greek. And when the New Testament speaks of the Lord Jesus Christ, the same word, "Kurios," is used.

Now the Watchtower Society — which denies the deity of Jesus Christ, and claims that if you don't use the word "Jehovah," God might not get your message — in their Bible arbitrarily translates "Kurios" sometimes into English "Lord," and other times back into Hebrew, "Jehovah." In Acts 19:5, the Word of God says, "When they heard this, they were baptized in the name of the Lord [Kurios] Jesus." In the Society's New World Translation it says, "On hearing this, they got baptized in the name of the Lord Jesus." If the Society were consistent in their translation they would have said "... in the name of Jehovah, Jesus."

In Romans 10:9, the Word says, "That if thou shalt confess with thy mouth the Lord [Kurios] Jesus, and shalt believe in thine heart that God hath raised him from the dead, thou shalt be saved." The Society's NWT says, "For if you publicly declare that 'word in your own mouth,' that Jesus is Lord, and exercise faith in your heart that God raised Him up from the dead, you will be saved." If they were consistent, they would have said ". . . believe that Jesus is Jehovah."

In Romans 10:13, still talking about the same Lord Jesus Christ, the Word of God says, "For whosoever shall call upon the name of the Lord [Kurios] shall be saved." This is a quotation from the Old Testament. The Watchtower Society puts in their translation, "For everyone who calls on the name of Jehovah will be saved." The subject is Jesus Christ the Lord. If you believe that Jesus is the Lord (Kurios) you'll be saved. And if you call upon the Lord (Kurios), you'll be saved. But there the Watchtower inconsistently inserts in their English translation the word "Jehovah" to fit their inconsistent doctrine.

Jesus in Revelation 1:8 said, "I am Alpha and Omega, the beginning and the ending, saith the Lord [Kurios]." But the Watchtower Society translates it " 'I am the Alpha and the Omega,' says Jehovah God, the One who is and who was and who is coming, the Almighty." Arbitrarily they change the speaker from Jesus to Jehovah. That's all right with me because Jesus is Jehovah. He is God. But it is not all right with the Society, because they believe in two gods, that Jehovah is one God, the Creator, and that Jesus is a secondary god, and a secondary creator.

Many centuries ago some Hebrew mystics decided that there was some intrinsic power in the tetragrammaton, YHVH. They theorized that they could make words, using only these four letters, and from these words make formulas and incantations that would have magical powers. They thought they had discovered an exclusive formula to tap into the spiritual power of God. Even today there exist ancient books of magic incantations, which originated from these Hebrew mystics. So-called Jehovah's Witnesses try to do the same thing.

They think, "We've got the exclusive formula. We know how to call on God and you don't, because *we* know how to pronouce the name in Hebrew." How do we know they know how to pronounce the name in Hebrew? How do we know it's not "Yahwe," instead of Jehovah? How do we know it's not something else entirely? Nobody knows. God said that the LORD will be His name forever. It can be in Hebrew, English, Spanish, French, Swahili, or any other language, or it can be in the language of the heart, not uttered.

The Jews were God's chosen people for more than one purpose. The primary purpose was to bring forth the Messiah. But another purpose was to be the keeper of the oracles, the revelation, of God. And we can certainly thank Israel today for keeping intact the Scriptures. We can thank the scribes of old who meticulously copied from one parchment to the other the Word of God. When the copyist scribes came to the word, "Elohim" (God), they stopped and washed their hands before copying it. When they came to the word "Adonai" (Lord), they stopped and washed their hands, then copied it. But when they came to the tetragrammaton, "YHVH" (LORD or Jehovah), they stopped and took a bath before copying it.

This name of God also teaches us about God. In Exodus, chapter 33, God spoke to Moses. Moses wanted to see God. But God told Moses he would not be allowed to see His face, but that God would put Moses in the cleft of the rock, and cover him there with His hand while God passed by. God said He would take away His hand and "thou shalt see my back parts: but my face shall not be seen."

Exodus 34:6-7: "And the LORD passed by before him, and proclaimed, The LORD [Jehovah, the Self-Existent One], The LORD God, merciful and gracious, longsuffering, and abundant in goodness and truth. Keeping mercy for thousands, forgiving iniquity and transgression and sin, and that will by no means clear the guilty; visiting the iniquity of the fathers upon the children, and upon the children's children, unto the third and to the fourth generation."

Moses got to see the "back parts" of God. This is an anthropomorphic expression; He was speaking to man in terms we could understand. God doesn't have a face; God is spirit; no man has seen God. But God said Moses could see His "back parts." I believe that what Moses saw with his eyes was the Shekinah, the glory cloud of God, which was a manifestation of the presence of God in a special way.

But I think Moses perceived the name of God, which spoke more fully of the attributes of God. He proclaimed to Moses, "The LORD," meaning He was eternal, self-existent, without beginning, and without end, and

—He was gracious;
—He was abundant in goodness and truth;
—He was forgiving, but He was just.
—He would by no means clear the guilty.
    The justice of God must be satisfied before God could be merciful, gracious, or longsuffering to the guilty.

How was the justice of God satisfied? By sending His Son, Jesus, to suffer and die on the cross as an atonement for our sins.

What is God's name? In the English language it is LORD, God, The Almighty, the Great I AM, Wonderful, Counselor, the Mighty God, the Everlasting Father, the Prince of Peace. Jesus mentioned three names of God in Matthew 28:19: ". . . the name of the Father, and of the Son, and of the Holy Ghost." Those who put so much stock in "Jehovah" as the only name for God, should take note too of what Jesus said in John 3:18, "He that believeth on him [speaking of Himself, Jesus, the Messiah] is not condemned: but he that believeth not is condemned already, because he hath not believed in the name of the only begotten Son of God."

16
What Happens to the Soul at Death?

In an attempt to prove the human soul does not continue in existence after death of the body, the Watchtower Society goes to great pains to prove that "animals as well as men are called souls," and that soul and spirit are not the same.

The Bible teaches that animals have souls, and that the soul and spirit are not the same, but it also teaches that the human soul does indeed continue in existence after death of the body. (There is no Bible doctrine, that I can find, regarding the continued existence of the animal soul one way or the other. Because of that we assume the animal soul does not continue.)

Without a religious hierarchy telling me what to believe or what to conclude, but based solely on Scripture, I believe the human being is body, soul, and spirit. I am body. I am soul. I am spirit. I spoke of my body when I told my wife, "I don't care what they do with me when I die; bury me, cremate me, or throw me out into the prairie for the coyotes to feed on." I spoke of my body as "me," and rightly so. But I also speak of my soul and my spirit as "me." After any of my usable organs or body parts have been utilized to help the living, and though the rest of my body is rotting in a grave, stored in an urn on the library shelf, or feeding the worms, buzzards, and coyotes on the prairie, "I" will not be present in that body, but will be present with the Lord who saved me.

Not everything the Society teaches about the soul

is false. Animals do have souls. You are a soul. Soul and spirit are not the same. But none of these prove that the soul ceases to exist at the death of the body.

In the Appendix of the Society's Bible, many statements are made about the soul, including:

1. The creature soul is mortal, destructible.
2. Soul delivered from Sheol (Hades, "hell").
3. Soul, a living person or creature.
4. Soul distinguished from spirit.

In Number 1, they use as a proof text, in NWT, Matthew 10:28: ". . . can destroy both soul and body in Gehenna . . ." Yet in Number 3, they suggest that body and soul are one and the same (though this thought is not spelled out). This is a good illustration of the compartmentalized thinking necessary to be a Jehovah's Witness. While thinking "Soul is a person, the same as the creature . . . your person and your body are the same, and the soul is your person . . ." he dares not think about the separation of body and soul spoken of in Number 1.

Let us see what the Bible teaches about the body, soul, and spirit.

I Thessalonians 5:23 says, "And the very God of peace sanctify you wholly; and I pray God your whole spirit and soul and body be preserved blameless unto the coming of our Lord Jesus Christ." Paul spoke to the Christians at Thessalonica as "you," persons; "you," who possess spirit and soul and body.

You are body. "And the LORD God formed man of the dust of the ground . . ." (Genesis 2:7). It was Adam's body that was formed out of the dust. Adam was body. ". . . for dust thou art, and unto dust shalt thou return" (Genesis 3:19). Adam (body) would return to dust.

It doesn't take much to convince a person that he

is flesh. If you have any doubt, give yourself a good pinch.

You are spirit. God "breathed into his nostrils the breath of life . . ." (Genesis 2:7). The Society *suggests* that the spirit of man is oxygen, on page 38 of their book, *The Truth That Leads to Eternal Life.*

On page 39 of the same book, is the following explanation of the spirit, "Whereas the human soul is the living person himself, the spirit is simply the life force that enables that person to be alive. The spirit has no personality, nor can it do the things a person can do. It cannot think, speak, hear, see or feel. In that respect, it might be likened to the electric current of a car's battery . . . ." The same page states flatly that men and animals have this same "life force or spirit."

This is a tenuous position in the light of mankind's special creation: "So God created man in his own image, in the image of God created he him; male and female created he them" (Genesis 1:27). How did God create man in His image? Does man look like God? No. "No man hath seen God at any time . . ." (John 1:18). Man was created a spirit being; it was in that respect that man was created in the image of God. "God is a Spirit" (John 4:24). God is not just oxygen, or just non-thinking electrical current. Neither is the spirit of man, which was created in the image of God.

It is the spirit of man that is born again when he is regenerated. "That which is born of the flesh is flesh; and that which is born of the Spirit is spirit. Marvel not that I said unto thee, Ye must be born again" (John 3:6-7).

The Word of God sheds the light we need on the doctrine of the Spirit of Man: God works through man's spirit: "The spirit of man is the candle of the LORD, searching all the inward parts . . ." (Proverbs 20:27).

The spirit of man has intelligence: "For what man

knoweth the things of a man, save the spirit of man which is in him? ..." (I Corinthians 2:11). It doesn't sound like oxygen or electricity to me!

The spirit of man has emotions: "When Jesus therefore saw her weeping, and the Jews also weeping which came with her, he groaned in the spirit, and was troubled" (John 11:33).

The spirit leaves the body at death: ". . . the body without the spirit is dead ..." (James 2:26). Jesus ". . . took her by the hand, and called, saying, Maid, arise. And her spirit came again, and she arose straightway ..." (Luke 8:54-55).

Although the Bible does not speak of the soul and spirit being divided one from another, such a division is possible. "For the word of God is quick, and powerful, and sharper than any twoedged sword, piercing even to the dividing asunder of soul and spirit ..." (Hebrews 4:12).

The soul, too, involves emotions. According to I Samuel 18:1, the souls of David and Jonathan were knit; Jonathan loved him as his own soul. According to II Samuel 5:8, David's soul hated the enemy. Job 14:22 says, ". . . his soul within him shall mourn."

Uninformed people have assumed that "animals don't have souls ... that's the difference between them and mankind ... animals can't love." Dogs love their masters. The lioness loves her cubs. A pet cat may in grief refuse to eat. Animals have souls, and they have emotions. There is no Bible evidence to indicate that they have spirits. The animals were not created in the image of God.

The soul feels sorrow: Jesus in the Garden of Gethsemane said, "My soul is exceeding sorrowful unto death" (Mark 14:34). The soul suffers: ". . . their soul is melted because of trouble" (Psalm 107:26). Speaking to Mary, the mother of Jesus, in the Temple, Simeon said, "Yea, a sword shall pierce through thy own soul also" (Luke 2:35).

The soul is clearly not something that goes into a grave and rots.

The soul and body are separated at death. In Zarephath, Zidon, the son of the widow who had fed Elijah died. Elijah "stretched himself upon the child three times, and cried unto the LORD, and said, O LORD, my God, I pray thee, let this child's soul come into him again. And the LORD heard the voice of Elijah; and the soul of the child came into him again, and he revived" (I Kings 17:21-22). Remember also that the ". . . body without the spirit is dead . . ." (James 2:26).

Man is not able to destroy the soul. He may kill the person by killing his body, and thereby cause the soul to be separated, but only God can destroy the soul, which does not necessitate annihilation of that soul. "And fear not them which kill the body, but are not able to kill the soul: but rather fear him which is able to destroy both soul and body in hell [Gehenna]" (Matthew 10:28).

The words "soul" and "person" are interchangeable, as are the words "body" and "person," and "spirit" and "person."

Revelation 19:20 and 20:10,15, have reference to unregenerate men who are resurrected, and then cast into the Lake of Fire to be destroyed eternally. They do not cease to exist, but are cast into the Lake of Fire where the Beast and False Prophet will have already been for 1,000 years. If the Lake of Fire meant annihilation rather than everlasting destruction involving conscious existence, the Beast and False Prophet would not last 1,000 years in its flame.

The soul, the person of the believer, is conscious after death: "Whether we wake or sleep, we should live together with him" (I Thessalonians 5:10). The Apostle Paul was speaking of believers. Whether the believer is alive on this earth or asleep in Jesus (death of the body) he lives with Christ. "We are confident, I say, and willing rather to be absent from the body, and to be present with the Lord" (II Corinthians 5:8). Neither of these scriptures suggest an unconscious existence, which point is further strengthened by Paul in Philippians 1:23: "For I am in a strait betwixt two, having a desire to depart, and to be with Christ; which is far better." The souls spoken of under the altar in heaven, in Revelation 6:9-10, speak, and therefore are conscious. They aren't corpses talking in their sleep.

The Sadducees, who denied the resurrection, asked Jesus about a man who died leaving no heirs, and whose widow married his seven brothers each in succession. Trying to trick Jesus, the Sadducees asked whose wife she would be in the resurrection. Jesus said there would be no marriage union, but people would be like the angels . . . . Are the angels not conscious? He said further, "But as touching the resurrection of the dead, have ye not read that which was spoken unto you by God, saying, I am the God of Abraham, and the God of Isaac, and the God of Jacob? God is not the God of the dead, but of the living" (Matthew 22:31-32). Those living are also conscious.

Luke 16, which has already been discussed, also definitely shows the conscious existence of the soul and spirit, the *person*, after death. The Society would have you believe that this chapter is a parable, and that the Lord used it to tell lies!

Lazarus died. The Bible doesn't say what happened to his body, but we assume it was taken to the Valley of Gehenna, the Jerusalem city dump, because Lazarus was a pauper and there were no funds for his burial. But though his body was eaten of worms, Lazarus went to Paradise.

The rich man died. His body was buried, but *he*, his soul and spirit, went to the realm of the dead, (Hades, hell) and was in torment; he cried to Abraham. The rich man was conscious. Lazarus was conscious. And so are all others who have died, regardless of the direction their *persons* went after being separate from their *bodies.*

The soul is precious: "For what shall it profit a man, if he shall gain the whole world, and lose his own soul? Or what shall a man give in exchange for his soul?" (Mark 8:36-37).

As a human being, created in the image of God, you are body, soul, and spirit; you are three, yet you are one. Efforts by faithless Watchtower apologists to disprove these truths are backed only by Bible verses taken *out of context*, and tricky verbal gymnastics. The Bible does not contradict itself, but it would have to be contradictory in order for the Society's claims to be true.

17

Then There Is "New Light"

To follow the Lord Jesus Christ's example by taking the gospel to people in their homes, I was visiting door-to-door in an apartment building. One door was answered by a middle-aged woman who, as soon as she heard my introduction, took a step backward, and while her eyes measured me, her lips made a practiced one-fourth of a smile, and she said confidently, "Thank you, I'm not interested. I have my own religion."

For an instant I saw my mother. Here was a dear person who had thought she was getting truth, but who had been brainwashed, and now responded like a robot.

"I have an idea what your religion is," I said.

"I'm one of Jehovah's Witnesses," she replied, and took another step back, half closing the door.

Hoping to penetrate some of the automated defenses built around her by the Society, and engage her in a person to person conversation, rather than just me talking and having her return conditioned responses, I said, "When I was a boy, the Witnesses believed theirs was not a religion . . . ."

"We have received a lot of *New Light* since then," was her conditioned response. She excused herself and closed the door.

When Charles Russell's Millennial Dawnists started, they believed they were born again and that they would go to heaven. As time went on they taught that only 144,000 altogether would make it, and urged prospective converts to get aboard before all the seats were taken.

When the 144,000 began to rapidly fill up, and new converts continued to be made, the Watchtower Society was in a dilemma. Like Joseph Smith, founder of Mormonism, who though already married, fell in love with a lovely 18-year-old girl, and received a "revelation from heaven" that polygamy was acceptable, Judge Joseph Rutherford, Russell's successor, received *New Light*: The 144,000 "Elect" would be the "Little Flock" and a great "Multitude" of other people could be recruited who would have no hope of heaven, but could look toward eternal life on earth. Newly invented doctrine was called *New Light*.

"Religion is a snare and a racket," was one of Rutherford's favorite slogans. But the most religious people on earth, the Witnesses, couldn't continue many generations claiming they weren't a religion, so the Society received *New Light*, and admitted it was indeed a religion.

The Society called its churches "ecclesias," (the Greek word translated "church") "companies," and "congregations," denying that they were churches. That made as much sense as saying, "My Buick is not an automobile; it's a car." So the Society later ended the embarrassment of brazen inconsistency by receiving *New Light*, and admitting theirs was a church. Discarding old doctrine was also *New Light*.

They claim Jesus Christ has been on earth personally ruling and reigning over His people through the Society since 1914. What an insult to the Lord, to suggest that He has to keep changing His mind and issuing contradictory *New Light* statements!

In the original charter of the Watch Tower Society of Pennsylvania, it states that the purposes of the Society include "public Christian worship of Almighty God and Jesus Christ." *New Light* has since told them that Jesus Christ is not the God, but is another god, and should not be worshiped. The Society's *New Light,* however does not change the true Word of God: "Let all the angels of God worship him" (Hebrews 1:6).

No man has the authority to add to the Word of God or to change it. Moses cautioned Israel, "What thing soever I command you, observe to do it; thou shalt not add thereto, nor diminish from it" (Deuteronomy 12:32).

The canon of Scripture was closed in Revelation 22:18-19: "For I testify unto every man that heareth the words of the prophecy of this book, If any man shall add unto these things, God shall add unto him the plagues that are written in this book: And if any man shall take away from the words of the book of this prophecy, God shall take away his part out of the book of life, and out of the holy city, and from the things which are written in this book."

God changes not: "I am the Lord, I change not" (Malachi 3:6). "Jesus Christ the same yesterday, and to day, and for ever" (Hebrews 13:8). "Every good gift and every perfect gift is from above, and cometh down from the Father of lights, with whom is no variableness, neither shadow of turning" (James 1:17).

God's Word changes not: "The grass withereth, the flower fadeth: but the word of our God shall stand for ever" (Isaiah 40:8). "Heaven and earth shall pass away, but my words shall not pass away" (Matthew 24:35). "For the prophecy came not in old time by the will of man: but holy men of God spake as they were moved by the Holy Ghost" (II Peter 1:21).

Those who add to God's Word are found to be liars: "Every word of God is pure: he is a shield unto them that put their trust in him. Add thou not unto his words, lest he reprove thee, and thou be found a liar" (Proverbs 30:5-6).

Each cult claims to be uniquely different; each

claims that its leadership has apostolic authority to make changes. The scriptural answer to these claims, in addition to the verses cited above, is found in Romans 16:17-18: "Now I beseech you, brethren, mark them which cause divisions and offences contrary to the doctrine which ye have learned; and avoid them. For they that are such serve not our Lord Jesus Christ, but their own belly; and by good words and fair speeches deceive the hearts of the simple." The doctrines of the Watchtower Society are certainly contrary to the doctrines Paul preached. The Christian should, therefore, avoid them who are so expert at good words and fair speeches, deceiving the hearts of the simple.

18
The Christian's Duty as a Citizen

The Witnesses have a lot of truth in their teachings, enough truth to disarm the unwary and make them receptive to their distinctive doctrines of error. For example, in the beginning of a book they might go to great pains to teach that the Bible is the Word of God, and that it only should be followed. Then later in the book they proceed to teach their own man-made doctrines. Similarly, some rat poison is ninety percent corn meal, perfectly harmless, and alone nourishing, but it contains enough poison to kill the rats.

Jehovah's Witnesses refuse to participate in normal acts of citizenship, such as voting. They refuse to salute the flag, and they refuse to serve in the Armed Forces. To those who ask why the Witnesses disobey a law, such as the draft law in wartime, one of the programmed answers is, "We obey man's law as long as it is not opposed to God's law." (I have said those words a thousand times.) Sometimes Biblical examples of godly people disobeying the law are cited.

There are rare cases in the Bible of man's law being violated by God's people. Shadrach, Meshach and Abednego refused to bow down to Nebuchadnezzar's golden idol, even though it was the law that they do so (Daniel 3:17-18). And their example was followed by thousands of martyrs in the early years of Christianity. But does that prove the Witnesses' point that Christians should not participate in government, and refuse to serve their country? Shadrach, Meshach and Abednego were high officials in the government of Babylon. They more than participated in the government.

Daniel disobeyed the law of the Medes and Persians, a law that had been designed specifically by his political enemies to entrap him and cause him to be cast into the lion's den. Daniel, a favorite of King Darius, was a high official in government, and Daniel's action certainly does not prove the Watchtower Society's points (Daniel 6:10).

Peter and John, who by the power of God healed a lame man at the Temple, and saw 5,000 people saved, were later ordered by the Sanhedrin to stop preaching (Acts 4:18-20). Naturally, Peter and John violated that order.

These cases are clear-cut. There was no room for doubt in the minds of the men of God who disobeyed these laws, nor would there be any doubt in the minds of Christians today who might be ordered to bow down to an idol, ordered not to pray, or ordered not to preach. Indeed there are Christians languishing in Russian jails today because they led their own children to Christ. There are Christian preachers in jails in India because it is illegal in some states there to cause anyone to change his religion.

The scriptural instruction to the Christian to obey civil government is specific. "Let every soul be subject unto the higher powers. For there is no power but of God: the powers that be are ordained of God. Whosoever therefore resisteth the power, resisteth the ordinance of God: and they that resist shall receive to themselves damnation. For rulers are not a terror to good works, but to the evil. Wilt thou then not be afraid of the power? do that which is good, and thou shalt have praise of the same: For he is the minister of God to thee for good. But if thou do that which is evil, be afraid; for he beareth not the sword in vain: for he is the minister of God, a revenger to execute wrath upon him that doeth evil. Wherefore ye must needs be subject, not only for wrath, but also for conscience sake. For for this cause pay ye tribute also: for they are God's ministers, attending continually upon this very thing. Render therefore to all their dues: tribute to whom tribute is due; custom to whom custom; fear to whom fear; honour to whom honour" (Romans 13:1-7).

We are to obey the magistrates (Titus 3:1). We are to submit to the ordinances of man (I Peter 2:13). We are not to just obey the laws we like, but all the laws. I hate to pay taxes, but I pay them. Jesus paid taxes (Matthew 17:27). He told us we should also pay taxes (Matthew 22:21).

War and killing are a part of this present evil world, and will be until the Lord Jesus Christ returns and sets up His kingdom and rules from Jerusalem (not Brooklyn as JWs state) in righteousness. A war is the same thing that happened between Cain and Abel on a much larger scale. If Abel had seen what was coming, he probably would have protected himself. If he had had certain knowledge that his brother planned to kill him, Abel might have made a preemptive strike.

One of the first wars recorded in the Bible involved Abraham, who marched against Chedorlaomer, king of Elam, leader of a five-nation confederacy that had sacked Sodom and Gomorrah. Though this war was small in comparison with a world war, it had many of the elements of any war. Abraham recruited other tribes to help him, Mamre, Eshcol, and Aner. Abraham had a standing army of three hundred trained men. They actually invaded a foreign land to pursue their enemies (Genesis 14:13-16). Did Abraham have to subscribe to all the evils of Sodom and Gomorrah to fight on their side? Abraham was fighting for his own people, Lot and his family.

Most fathers, even those under Watchtower discipline, understand why it would be necessary to defend their own families and their own homes. They can also understand why a community of families might band together for common protection. (I have seen the Witnesses in action in this regard at the Watchtower Conventions, when hundreds of "ushers" were issued heavy oak walking canes and posted in strategic locations around the convention site to prevent disturbances by hecklers.)

A nation is simply a large tribe, or a large community. The principles are the same. There are many things that happen in our country and in our government that I deplore, but it is still the best and most godly nation on earth, and I have more people in this land than Abraham had in Sodom; and I, as a part of this larger community, have a responsibility to do my proportionate share in its protection, and so does everyone else.

There is an Old Testament precedent for the military draft. In Israel, every man, age twenty and older was drafted (Numbers 1:30). There were exceptions for temporary exemptions, one of which was if a man were "fearful and fainthearted" (Deuteronomy 20:5-8). The draft in Israel continued throughout that nation's history, and continues today. (Israel today has real equality of the sexes; both men and women must serve.) The argument that Israel was God's people, and therefore the military draft there was unique, just won't hold water. Israel was not always following the will of God; Israel's kings, who led in battle, were not always following the will of God.

If God's will had been for men to refuse military service, or if it had been His will for those in military service to desert, He would surely have mentioned it someplace in His Word. But the opposite is true.

John the Baptist's advice to soldiers involved the honest discharge of their duty. "And the soldiers likewise demanded of him, saying, And what shall we do?" The Society, if given the opportunity, would have advised them to refuse to obey orders and go to jail! But John said, "Do violence to no man, neither accuse any falsely; and be content with your wages" (Luke 3:14). John's advice in no way resembled the dogmatic demands put upon the disciples of the Watchtower. John's allusion was to soldiers who did violence, or intimidated people and extorted money from them by force. During that period of history, soldiers would often become discontented, especially over lack of pay, or insufficient wages or rations, and would mutiny. John cautioned them against it: "Be content with your wages," he said.

When Jesus was in Capernaum, a Roman centurian, an officer over a hundred men, beseeched Him to heal his servant, saying, "Speak the word only, and my servant shall be healed. For I am a man under authority, having soldiers under me; and I say to this man, Go, and he goeth; and to another, Come, and he cometh; and to my servant, Do this, and he doeth it." What would the Society's attitude be to such an officer? They would certainly want to offer him up as a sacrifice to *persecution* publicity. But Jesus "marvelled, and said to them that followed, Verily I say unto you, I have not found so great faith, no, not in Israel" (Matthew 8:5-10).

Secular history tells us that one of the reasons Christianity spread so rapidly was because of the many Roman soldiers who became Christians; and as they were transferred, spread their faith to the far reaches of the Empire.

The Apostle Peter also had dealings with soldiers. Another centurion, Cornelius, was saved and, along with his entire household, was baptized. Peter never advised Cornelius to quit being a soldier (Acts 10:7).

The Society's favorite proof text on the military service question, John 18:36, they use out of context: "Jesus answered, My kingdom is not of this world: if my kingdom were of this world, then would my servants fight . . . ." Here is where they stop quoting, and say this proves men should go to prison rather than to military service. Jesus was explaining why His servants did not fight to prevent Him from being taken to be put to death. ". . . if my kingdom were of this world, then would my servants fight, that I should not be delivered to the Jews: but now is my kingdom not from hence."

Jesus came to the earth for the purpose of dying on the cross for our sins. He said, "I lay down my life, that I might take it again. No man taketh it from me, but I lay it down of myself. I have power to lay it down, and I have power to take it again" (John 10:17-18). His refusal to let His servants fight to prevent His arrest has nothing whatever to do with civil disobedience, refusing military service, or lack of participation in common acts of citizenship.

John the Baptist was asked by tax collectors, "Master, what shall we do?" He didn't tell them to quit their "civil service" jobs and take no active part in government: "And he said unto them, Exact no more than that which is appointed you" (Luke 3:12-13).

If Christians are to be the "salt of the earth" as Jesus said, they must participate in the political process (Matthew 5:13). Jesus was alluding to salting meat to preserve it. The salt is the difference between a savory slice of ham and rotten meat. Christians seeking to live by the ideals set forth by Jesus in His Sermon on the Mount, and setting up these and other Biblical rules of conduct as criteria for a godly government and community, serve as the salt of the earth to prevent rot.

If Christian citizens do not vote against wrong at every opportunity, they are giving tacit approval to it. If Christians do not try to elect men like Abraham, Shadrach, Meshach, Abednego, and Daniel to public office, they become parties to unprincipled government.

19
The Literal Return
of Jesus Christ

During one of my visits to my parents, my step-father asked the blessing on the food at a meal, "... in the Name of our present ruling King, Christ Jesus ...." I asked that he explain the remark in his prayer. He said emphatically that Jesus Christ is now ruling and reigning through His people, the Jehovah's Witnesses, and that He had been doing so since 1914.

There are many different ideas about the Second Coming of Jesus Christ. You hear terms like amillennial, premillennial, and postmillennial. These usually indicate differences of opinion between Christians, people who are trusting in Jesus Christ as Lord and Saviour, but they disagree on how He will come the second time. I am a premillennialist; I believe that Jesus Christ will return, and will set up an earthly kingdom and personally rule and reign here for a thousand years. Certainly a person can disagree with others about the return of Jesus Christ, and still be saved. But I believe that if a person reads the Bible, and believes what the Bible says, that he's going to believe that Jesus Christ *will return.*

Some few people believe that the world is just going to keep on getting better and better, that Christianity will eventually become worldwide and that we will usher in the millennial kingdom; "we're going to make the earth fit for Jesus, and He will come back and reign"—that is the postmillennial position. Many people had that idea, but left it when they saw in World War I and World War II that modern man can be more cruel than mankind had ever been, and that instead of mankind evolving into a better and higher creature, we are "devolving" morally in the opposite direction.

Another school of thought, amillennialism, believes there will be no millennial kingdom; the scriptures that have to do with His return and rule are just "spiritualized" into nothingness.

I believe Jesus Christ will return and set up a government of righteousness on the throne of David in Jerusalem—that everything will be right about the government. (Imagine that! Perfect and just government is something we're not used to.) The prophecy in Isaiah 9:6 will be fulfilled, "For unto us a child is born, unto us a son is given: and the government shall be upon his shoulder: and his name shall be called Wonderful, Counsellor, The mighty God, The everlasting Father, The Prince of Peace." Jesus will return, and will reign with His saints a thousand years. This is the premillennial position.

Others believe Jesus will return, but not literally and physically. They also believe necessarily that He did not rise literally and physically from the dead. I think this is a demonstrated lack of faith, unbelief, because the Bible teaches that Jesus did literally and physically rise from the grave.

When the women came to anoint the body of Jesus that had been buried in the sepulchre, they found that the stone had been rolled away from the cave entrance. An angel said to them, "Why seek ye the living among the dead? He is not here, but is risen" (Luke 24:5-6). They did not say, "His body is lying in there rotting in the grave, but He himself has been spiritually wafted away." The angels were talking about something that physically happened.

Paul said ". . . that he was buried, and that he rose again the third day . . ." (I Corinthians 15:4). The same "he" that was buried was also resurrected. It was by the power of the Spirit of God that He was resurrected, but the same one regained life that had lost life.

If Christ's being raised by the Spirit was not a physical resurrection, then neither will the resurrection of His people be physical: "But if the Spirit of him that raised up Jesus from the dead dwell in you, he that raised up Christ from the dead shall also quicken your mortal bodies by his Spirit that dwelleth in you" (Romans 8:11). The believer's resurrection will be the same kind of resurrection as was Jesus'. "For if we believe that Jesus died and rose again, even so them also which sleep in Jesus will God bring with him" (I Thessalonians 4:14).

After Jesus was resurrected from the grave, He went up to Galilee and met with the disciples as He had told them before He was crucified. Five hundred saw Him at one time (I Corinthians 15:6).

Another time, his disciples were frightened, supposing they had seen a spirit, but Jesus reassured them and asked them to "Handle me and see; for a spirit hath not flesh and bones, as ye see me have" (Luke 24:39). Jesus was telling the disciples and demonstrating to them that He was not just spirit, but that He was physically, literally alive from the dead.

When the Society claims the opposite, somebody's lying, and it's not Jesus! He asked them for food. In His resurrected and glorified body He ate broiled fish and honeycomb (Luke 24:42). (If you like to eat as much as I do, you too will be pleased to realize that this indicates that there will be eating in heaven.) This Jesus was not some kind of invisible, unreal spirit floating around. This was physical flesh and bones.

The Watchtower Society denies the physical resurrection of Jesus Christ, and they deny His physical return. Charles Taze Russell, the cult's founder, put them out on a limb when he said positively that Jesus would return in 1914. It was a source of great embarrassment for the Russellites, when Jesus Christ didn't show. So later, in order to salvage their honor, they said Jesus did indeed return in 1914; we just didn't see Him.

Such "spiritualizing" is like a common attempt to comfort the surviving wife whose husband has died.

"Oh, he isn't dead. He's still with us—in spirit." That is little comfort to the grieving widow. She watched the remains lowered into the grave. She went home to an empty house. If her husband is still around in spirit, she can't see him, touch him, or hear him. He no longer holds her and comforts her. He doesn't bring home a paycheck anymore. His memory may be there, but *he* is gone.

The Watchtower Society, which insists on judging the doctrine of the Trinity with rationale (straining at a gnat), quickly closes that compartment in its thinking, and opens a new one, propagating the belief that Jesus Christ is personally ruling the earth, and has been since 1914 (swallowing a camel).

The Spirit of God indwells every believer. Every believer has the Spirit of Christ. So in a "spiritual" sense, Christ is still here with us; He never left! "... If any man have not the Spirit of Christ, he is none of his" (Romans 8:9).

Let's examine what Jesus said about His second coming: "Immediately after the tribulation of those days shall the sun be darkened, and the moon shall not give her light, and the stars shall fall from heaven, and the powers of the heavens shall be shaken: And then shall appear the sign of the Son of man in heaven: and then shall all the tribes of the earth mourn, and they shall see the Son of man coming in the clouds of heaven with power and great glory" (Matthew 24:29-30). These things did not happen in 1914.

179

Verse 27 of the same chapter says, "For as the lightning cometh out of the east, and shineth even unto the west; so shall also the coming of the Son of man be." Jesus taught that people would see Him when He returns. He taught that it would be after a great tribulation unlike the world has ever seen. When Jesus said ". . . and they shall see the Son of man coming . . ." that is exactly what He meant.

He said ". . . I will come again, and receive you unto myself; that where I am, there ye may be also" (John 14:3). None of Christ's statements about His return in glory to rule the earth indicate secrecy, but rather the opposite. For a small group of men in a suite of offices in Brooklyn, New York, to claim in twenty-six languages that Jesus is now present, ruling through them, and speaking through them, is blasphemy.

Let's examine what the angels said about Jesus' second coming. As the disciples watched Him go up into the cloud, the angels said, "This same Jesus . . . shall so come in like manner as ye have seen him go into heaven" (Acts 1:11). This same Jesus whom they had handled, who had eaten with them, who positively stated that He was not spirit but was flesh and bones, ascended up into heaven before their eyes. They saw a literal, living, glorified Christ rise. His second coming will be as His ascension, literal, physical, and visible.

Getting any other "interpretation" from this passage of scripture than what it plainly says is like "interpreting" the meaning of a stop sign. Try that on a traffic policeman or a municipal judge. If the Society leaders interpreted man's law like they do God's, they would all be in jail.

Imagine a person going through a stop sign, and explaining to the traffic policeman, "We all have our ways of interpreting these signs." Or you might sometime try going seventy miles an hour in a fifty miles per hour zone, and explain to the judge, "In spirit, I was only doing fifty."

The angels positively said Jesus would return, as He left: physically, literally.

Let's examine what the Old Testament prophets said about Christ's second coming. The LORD (Jehovah) said in Zechariah 12:10, ". . . and they shall look upon me whom they have pierced . . . ." Christ was pierced. And after His resurrection He invited doubting Thomas to thrust his hand into Jesus' side that had been pierced by the Roman spear. Those people who pierced Jesus will look upon Him when He resurrects them and judges them. They will see Him because He will literally return.

According to Zechariah 14:4, the LORD's feet shall stand on the Mount of Olives, from which place the Lord Jesus Christ arose. "And his feet shall stand in that day upon the mount of Olives, which is before Jerusalem on the east, and the mount of Olives shall cleave in the midst thereof toward the east and toward the west, and there shall be a very great valley; and half of the mountain shall remove toward the north, and half of it toward the south." These events have not yet occurred. Yet the angels said the Lord Jesus would return as He left. So we can look forward to Jesus returning, setting foot back on the Mount of Olives, and the mount will split and divide, in fulfillment of the prophecy. That didn't happen in 1914.

Let's examine what the inspired apostles said of Christ's second coming. Paul said, ". . . Keep this commandment without spot, unrebukeable, until the appearing of our Lord Jesus Christ: Which in his times he shall shew, who is the blessed and only Potentate, the King of kings, and Lord of lords . . ." (I Timothy 6:14-15). Regardless of the verbal gymnastics perpetrated by the Watchtower Society, "appearing" still means "appearing," and His "presence" does not suggest invisibility, but quite the opposite. People will see Him. He will rule as King of kings, which is not now taking place, and Lord of lords. John said in Revelation 1:7 "... and every eye shall see him ...."

20
Put on the Armor of God

How should the Christian deal with Jehovah's Witnesses? First, he should not in any way encourage them. "Whosoever transgresseth, and abideth not in the doctrine of Christ, hath not God. He that abideth in the doctrine of Christ, he hath both the Father and the Son. If there come any unto you, and bring not this doctrine, receive him not into your house, neither bid him God speed: For he that biddeth him God speed is partaker of his evil deeds" (II John 9-11).

Without giving aid and comfort to the enemy, and without encouraging heresy, we can effectively witness to the *Witnesses;* we can tell the truth about *The Truth.* But in order to do so we must have the "whole armour of God." Don't go into battle without it:

Put on the whole armour of God, that ye may be able to stand against the wiles of the devil.

For we wrestle not against flesh and blood, but against principalities, against powers, against the rulers of the darkness of this world, against spiritual wickedness in high places.

Wherefore take unto you the whole armour of God, that ye may be able to withstand in the evil day, and having done all, to stand.

Stand therefore, having your loins girt about with truth, and having on the breastplate of righteousness;

And your feet shod with the preparation of the gospel of peace;

Above all, taking the shield of faith, wherewith ye shall be able to quench all the fiery darts of the wicked.

And take the helmet of salvation, and the sword of the Spirit, which is the word of God (Ephesians 6:11-17).

False doctrines of the Watchtower Society are "wiles of the devil." These false doctrines serve as a substitute for truth. They are a way other than the "straight and narrow way," Jesus Christ. All other plans of salvation, including the Watchtower's work plan, are on the "broad way, that leadeth to destruction" (Matthew 7:13-14). Wily Satan doesn't care which substitute for the true gospel of Christ is used, just as long as people stay away from the narrow gate, Christ, the way to eternal life. Every person has a void in his· heart that Jesus Christ will exactly fit. The cults have substitutes that don't exactly fit, but they serve to keep out Christ.

The Society's doctrine that you must work, work, work, publish, publish, publish, witness, witness, witness, in order to have an opportunity for salvation is "another gospel," which Paul cautioned against in Galatians 1:6-8. If the Pope in Rome, the Twelve Mormon Apostles in Salt Lake City, the Watchtower Society in Brooklyn, the preacher who baptized you, or your white-haired grandfather, preach any other gospel, let him be accursed.

The wiles of the devil, promulgated by the Watchtower Society, include verbal gymnastics. The Christian should stand against them, ready to fight, and be determined to lose no ground. Some of the examples of their verbal gymnastics we have already seen, such as using the Hebrew word instead of the English word—*gehenna* instead of hell, and *Jehovah* instead of LORD. Another example of the Society's verbal gymnastics is in the word "cross."

Because the cross has been wrongly venerated by

professing Christians, the Society strains at a gnat to try to prove that Jesus was not put to death on a cross. They cite Acts 5:30, and 10:39 where the cross is called a "tree." They cite obscure writings of a few who supposed that Jesus died on an upright pole without a cross-member. What's the difference? The shape of the cross has no bearing on Christ's sacrificial death. Those prone to idolatry would have venerated a single pole, a hangman's noose, or an electric chair. The Society implies that *Christendom*, the one apostate pot into which they dump all professing Christians, has some paganistic, mystic attachment to the shape of the cross! "Ridiculous," you say? I agree. But there is a brainwashed multitude that believes such nonsense.

The Greek word translated "cross" meant "a stake, post, pole, or cross." The Society has chosen instead of *cross*, "torture stake," and used that term in their Bible. Their use of "torture stake" instead of "cross" is not inaccurate, per se. Neither would "post" have been inaccurate, or "pole," or "tree." But their translation is misleading and dishonest. It is one of their many attempts to discredit orthodox Christianity in any way possible.

Jesus was crucified on a Roman cross, which according to unquestionable historic accounts from many sources, was shaped just like the traditional cross. The Society seeks documentation for its far-out doctrines from world literature, and lifts sentences and paragraphs to prove their position from works that are otherwise opposed to the Watchtower doctrines. The Society lifts these items from world literature like it lifts verses out of the Bible. For every ounce of obscure opinions the Society uses to document a *stake* without a cross-piece, there is a ton of documentation to prove the cross was a *cross*.

A senseless attack on something as insignificant as the design of the cross has the same psychological purpose to the Society that argument over the shape of the conference table had to the Vietnamese communists at the Paris Peace Talks. Neither the Society nor the communists are stupid; they are wily, and their wiles are guided and coordinated by Satan.

The Christian should stand ready to contend for the faith: "Ye should earnestly contend for the faith which was once delivered unto the saints" (Jude 3).

How can the Christian defend himself from the wiles of the devil, and contend for the faith at the same time? He can put on the whole armor of God.

Our loins are to be "girt with truth." In Bible times both men and women wore long skirts, which got in the way when they wanted to run, work, or fight. The girdle, or wide belt of linen or leather worn around the waist, served to hold up the skirt to a much more manageable, shorter length. The girding of the loins, tucking the long skirt up under the girdle, so it wouldn't get in the way, is, in the armor of God, a picture of truth.

Without the truth our fight is hampered. We must make sure of our facts. Because of a lack of truth in its false doctrines, the Society is continually "stepping on its skirt." Its false doctrines, and dishonest misrepresentation of truth get in its way. The truth "girdle" is both defensive and offensive. As a possessor of real truth, you need not be confused by claims of *The Truth*.

The "breastplate of righteousness" is a defensive piece of armor, turning back the arrow, spear, and sword. But where can we obtain righteousness? Isaiah 64:6 tells us that all our righteousnesses are as filthy rags, worse than worthless. Jesus said our righteousness must exceed the righteousness of the scribes and Pharisees (Matthew 5:20). These were the most outwardly righteous people on earth. They prayed. They tithed. They fasted. They made a big show of outwardly following the Law of Moses, and their own nit-picking additions to it, beyond the letter and the jot and tittle.

Righteous living is a sign of inward righteousness and a sign of the new birth. "If ye know that he is righteous, ye know that every one that doeth righteousness is born of him" (I John 2:29).

In order to defend oneself from Watchtower brainwashing, one must possess the breastplate of righteousness, which comes only from Christ. One must also demonstrate that he possesses that breastplate of righteousness by righteous living.

Our feet must be shod with the "preparation of the gospel of peace." The soldier can do little without protection for his feet from rocky ground, thorns, and debris of battle. The feet being shod serves both defensively and offensively, as the gospel is defensive and offensive, in protecting the Christian, in actively opposing false doctrine, and in bringing others to a saving knowledge of Jesus Christ. When one has believed the gospel, and trusted in the Lord Jesus Christ, he should have peace.

Peace is one thing the Witnesses don't have. Members of the *little flock* have no assurance that they won't become *unprofitable servants* and lose their place in the 144,000 *elect*. The *Jonadab multitude* have no assurance they will ever merit eternal life; members of neither group have assurance that they will be able to *endure faithfully to the end*. When a loved one dies in the Watchtower faith, his fellow-Witnesses have no assurance they will ever again have fellowship with him. One or the other of them might be separated as *goats* on the day of judgment, and no one will know for sure until then!

I tried to explain to my mother the peace of Christ. It was like trying to explain a rainbow to a man born blind; she didn't understand. Her life was filled with anxiety.

The little old lady that sat me down in a pew in a rescue mission and tried to lead me to Jesus, wasn't trying to gain points so *she* could get to heaven. She *already* had a home in heaven. She was trying to get *me* there. When my wife's uncle Fritz spent three hours in a tactless but sincere effort to win me to Christ, he was doing it out of compassion for me. My wife who prayed, and my father-in-law, who reasoned with me out of Scripture and invited me to church, were not working for "points," trying to get a foot in heaven's door. The preacher who led me to Christ was not using me as a ladder for himself, trying to claw his way over heaven's wall, but witnessed to me because he wanted me to have the gift of God. But when a Witness knocks on your door, he is trying to build up "points" in heaven, hoping that if he puts in enough time, files enough reports, has enough *book studies,* and *back calls,* suffers *persecution,* and *endures faithfully to the end,* he might get to live on earth eternally. He does not have the gospel of peace, nor can he offer it.

If you are to deal with the brainwashed, *you* must have the gospel of peace. If you are truly saved and living for the Lord, you can know it and have assurance: "He that believeth on him is not condemned: but he that believeth not is condemned already, because he hath not believed in the name of the only begotten Son of God" (John 3:18). God said it; believe it! "He that believeth on the Son hath everlasting life: and he that believeth not the Son shall not see life; but the wrath of God abideth on him" (verse 36).

Above all we must have the "shield of faith." This suggests not a small, round shield, used by light infantry, but a heavy, large, oblong shield that covers the entire body. Above all we must have faith before we can successfully defend ourselves against Watchtower brainwashing.

"So then faith cometh by hearing, and hearing by the word of God" (Romans 10:17). How do you get more faith? By reading the Word of God, by hearing the Word of God. In order for a person to be a Jehovah's Witness, and continue in that doctrine, he must have regular doses of *Watchtower*. Russell admitted that if a person read the Bible alone, he would not continue in the Watchtower doctrine. The defense against the flaming arrows of Satan that come knocking on your door, is the shield of faith. The more you read and hear the Word of God, the more your faith grows. Christian literature is fine and helpful, but don't let it take the place of the Bible.

All other defensive measures are useless if the soldier is hit on his unprotected head. We must, therefore, have the "helmet of salvation." No matter how much Bible or theology a person knows, if he does not personally possess salvation, he is vulnerable to attack. Many who profess to be Christians are not really saved. This is why the Society can attack *Christendom* and we can't argue with many things the Society says against Christendom, because they are true. More is involved in being a Christian than saying, "I'm a Christian." More is involved than walking down the aisle of a church and shaking a preacher's hand.

Jesus said, "Not everyone that saith unto me, Lord, Lord, shall enter into the kingdom of heaven; but he that doeth the will of my Father which is in heaven. Many will say to me in that day, Lord, Lord, have we not prophesied in thy name? and in thy name have cast out devils? and in thy name done many wonderful works? And then will I profess unto them, I never knew you: depart from me, ye that work iniquity" (Matthew 7:21-23).

Be sure you really have the helmet of salvation. If there is any doubt that you have accepted Christ, and claimed God's promises of salvation, do it now.

Not only is the Christian to have protective armor against the wiles of the devil, but he is also to have offensive weaponry, the "sword of the Spirit, which is the word of God." Read it. Believe it. Practice it. Propagate it. There is no substitute for the pure, "un-commented-on" Word of God.

Jehovah's Witnesses don't know the Word of God. They know the parts that have been programmed into their brainwashed minds. Their conditioned responses are well-oiled and functional. But they have not read the Word of God and understood it as they would read and understand the meaning of any other book, because the Society has not allowed it. So if the Christian has the "sword of the Spirit," he has the advantage of those who only have the out-of-context proof texts, as it were, fiery darts shot off in all directions.

The only way the Witness can use his flaming arrows to advantage, is to concentrate them toward one point against the unarmed unbeliever, or the inadequately armed believer. How can this be avoided? Make him stay on the subject. If you are trying to win a Witness to Christ, don't let him control the conversation. If you want to tell your personal testimony, and explain the new birth, and salvation, don't let him switch to *Christendom, Armageddon, Jehovah, Hell,* and *Soul,* and back again. Stick with the new birth and salvation. You can always deal with the other subjects later. And when you decide one subject has been exhausted, and go to another, preferably on another occasion, stick with the chosen subject. Try to break through the Watchtower wall, and get him to think for himself. Remember, the brainwashed Witness has not thought these things out for himself; he is giving programmed responses. Use the Word of God, the sword of the Spirit. God will do with it what no man can do with brilliant arguments or eloquence.

We should never advocate laws against the free exercise of any religion, regardless of how heretical (with the possible exception of religious activity that is harmful to others, such as causing the death of an innocent child by refusing to allow a blood transfusion). Laws used against the cults can also be used against genuine and harmless Christians.

Don't be bitter against a brainwashed individual because of the evil his masters propagate. Instead, love him as Christ loved him, and pray for him. Pray for him privately when you are alone; pray for him in Christian groups; pray for him in his presence. Let him know you are praying for him. I have often told Witnesses that I would pray for them, and with only one exception, my mother, they have said to the effect: "No, thank you. I'll do my own praying." We should pray anyway, however, remembering, "The effectual fervent prayer of a righteous man availeth much" (James 5:16).

God loves the Witnesses as He loves every sinner who needs Christ. Christ died for the Witnesses just as He did for the Hindus, Buddhists, Moslems, and unregenerate members of Christian churches. "For God so loved the world . . . ." That love includes the victims of Watchtower brainwashing.